THE ANATOMY OF

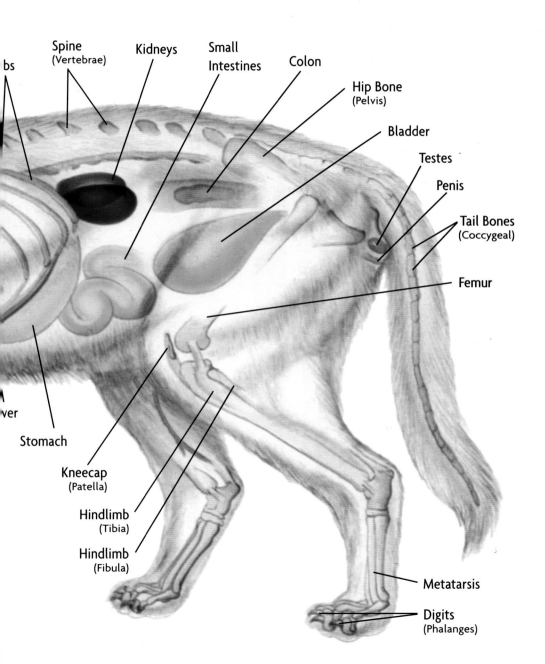

bs

Spine
(Vertebrae)

Kidneys

Small
Intestines

Colon

Hip Bone
(Pelvis)

Bladder

Testes

Penis

Tail Bones
(Coccygeal)

Femur

ver

Stomach

Kneecap
(Patella)

Hindlimb
(Tibia)

Hindlimb
(Fibula)

Metatarsis

Digits
(Phalanges)

Cornish Rex Cat

◇

By Eve Denise Jones

CONTENTS

PUBLISHED IN THE UNITED KINGDOM BY:

INTERPET
PUBLISHING

Vincent Lane, Dorking   Surrey RH4 3YX   England

ISBN 1-84286-047-X

PHOTO CREDITS
Photography by Isabelle Français and Alan Robinson
with additional photographs by Michael W Brim,
Cat Fanciers Association, Carolina Biological Supply,
Fleabusters Rx for Fleas, James R Hayden, RBP, Interpet, Dwight R Kuhn,
Dr Dennis Kunkel, Mikki Pet Products, Phototake, Jean Claude Revy, Erin
Winters and WB Saunders Company.

The publisher would like to thank all of the owners of the cats featured
in this book, including Donna & Richard Gonyea and Paul & Dolores Spivack.

CORNISH REX CAT

Cornwall is a county with a breathtakingly beautiful and rugged coastline, a land where fairy tales and legends rub shoulders with reality. The source of inspiration for artists, poets and novelists, parts of its hinterland are also famed for their bleakness, especially during the winter months. Nowhere is this more evident than on the higher elevations of Bodmin Moor, with its freezing misty nights, marshes and bogs.

It is on the edge of this small, yet remote, wilderness that the first rex-coated mutation to be developed as a breed was discovered in a barnyard cat. Strange things happen in Cornwall, and, as you will discover, the development of this beautiful breed certainly had more than its share of the mysterious, the unusual, the foolhardy and the sorrowful surrounding it.

KALLIBUNKER

The cat that was to become the father of the Cornish Rex was called Kallibunker. He was a cream kitty born on 21 July 1950, one of five kittens in a litter from

THE REX COAT

The normal cat coat is comprised of three hair types: guard, awn and down. The guard hairs are the longest, thickest and most coarse in texture. The awn hairs (also called bristle) are shorter as well as thinner. The guard and awn hairs create what is called the topcoat. The topcoat creates a weather-resistant barrier to protect the down hairs against rain, ice, snow and temperature fluctuations, be these hot or cold.

The down hairs are the shortest, thinnest and softest. They display a slight wave along their length and are known collectively as the undercoat or underfur. Their role, as in the down feathers of birds, is to trap warm air. The three hair types display a range, meaning there is a gradual change from one type to the next.

The rex mutation has the effect of removing the guard hairs while causing the awn hairs to become shorter, softer and curled or wavy. They appear much like down hairs but are very smooth. The Cornish Rex's whiskers display variable degrees of curl, but are much more normal than those of the Devon Rex.

a domestic female farm cat. Her name was Serena. She was a normal-coated tortoiseshell (tortie) and white, owned by Mrs Nina Ennismore.

Kalli's father was unknown, but, in order to produce Kalli, he had to be at the least both a Rex and a dilute gene carrier. Given this fact, while Kallibunker was the first Cornish Rex mutant to be identified and bred from, the mutation that created his unique looks must have dated probably from the 1940s.

At this point, it should be mentioned that some authors have stated that Kalli was a red tabby, while Serena was a tortie rather than a tortie and white. According to the records of Mrs Ennismore, Kalli was a cream and Serena was a tortie and white. It can be added that the colours of some other of the early cats have been the source of dispute as well.

Certain of the early records of Mrs Ennismore were lost, while others left a great deal to be desired. With these facts in mind, we will not dwell on them. They are peripheral topics best left to larger, more detailed, texts.

These digressions stated, Mrs Ennismore noticed that Kallibunker was unusual in that his coat displayed curls and waves rather than normal straight feline fur. She also noticed his bodily structure was rather unusual. He was more lithe, and his head was of the type known in cat circles as 'foreign,' which means that it had a wedge look to it, as compared to the fuller cheeks and round appearance of the domestic moggie. However, at that time, nothing further was done with Kalli. He therefore spent the first two years of his life running around the farmyard being 'one of the boys' and plying his trade as a catcher of mice, as well as being a favoured pet. It is with his pet status in mind that Mrs Ennismore decided to neuter him.

colour varieties, in particular the Colourpoint Longhair (Persian). The mating of Kalli and Serena produced three kittens. Two of these did not survive, which left a blue-cream and white male that was given the name of Poldhu.

POLDHU

There are three reasons why Poldhu is deserving of special attention in the history of the Cornish Rex, and indeed of the cat fancy. One obviously is that he became the first sire in the breed after Kallibunker. The second is that he was a blue-cream, which is the dilution of tortoiseshell. This pattern is exceedingly rare in males and is created by a genetic anomaly.

But by far the most important aspect was that he proved to be a fertile cat, when the vast majority of male torties are sterile. Poldhu sired a number of litters. It has been suggested that he was actually a blue tabby and white. However, if this were so, it is unlikely that this fact would have escaped the attention of the vet, the geneticist Dr A G Searle and of Brian Sterling-Webb, who was later to become Poldhu's owner.

The vet and Dr Searle persuaded Mrs Ennismore to allow them to effect a minor operation so that they could take a testicle sample for microscopic study. Poldhu recovered without problem from the 'minor' surgery

There is no limit to the colours, combinations and patterns in which the Cornish Rex can be seen. This is a lovely blue and white.

THE BREED BEGINS

When Kallibunker was taken to the surgery, the vet suggested to Mrs Ennismore that he should be bred in order to establish more information on his unique type. A well-known geneticist of the day, Albert C Jude was subsequently contacted. At his suggestion, Kalli was confined and mated to his mother.

Another expert was also contacted. He was Brian Sterling-Webb, well known for his experimental breeding to establish new

WHAT'S IN A NAME?

The name 'Rex' was originally applied to the Castor Rex mutation in rabbits, following its development as a breed in France during 1919 (though the mutation was known for many years prior to this). 'Castor' is derived from the Greek word *kastor*, meaning 'beaver.' 'Rex' is derived from the Latin word meaning 'king.'

With the passage of years, other rexoid mutations appeared in rabbits and various other mammals, and the term 'Rex' became a broad term to cover all of these. Used alone, it refers to the plush velvet-like coat of the rabbit breed simply called the Rex. Mrs Nina Ennismore is said to have been a breeder of Rex rabbits and she saw this same unusual hair on Kallibunker, a kitten born to her female farm cat Serena. This is why she used the term *Rex* (though it may have been at the suggestion of Albert C Jude, a well-known geneticist of the day).

Originally the Cornish Rex was simply called the English Rex, or sometimes, more commonly, the Poodle Rex. However, the later discovery of the Devon Rex necessitated a change, and so the two forms were identified by their respective counties of origin.

but never sired another litter, and the sample taken from him was lost!

Poldhu was but one example of what seems to be a catalogue of disasters that was to befall the breed's early years. Three females paired to Poldhu after his operation failed to conceive and were declared by the vet to be sterile and were put to sleep. Many of the first Rex hybrid carriers were destroyed until Mrs Ennismore was persuaded to retain them for their future breeding value.

EARLY PROBLEMS

Apart from the loss of Poldhu as a sire, another major problem during the early years was the high mortality rate in litters, sometimes the entire litter. Mrs Ennismore felt this was a consequence of the intense inbreeding she was advised to undertake in order for the English Rex to reach the needed number of generations to qualify for breed status.

While close inbreeding is a prerequisite (and beneficial) in any developing breed, its downside is what is known as inbreeding depression. This is the bringing together of harmful genes that ordinarily would not come together in a larger genetic pool, in which the degree of relationships is less close. Another consequence of inbreeding is it

An example of the tortoiseshell pattern, commonly referred to as 'tortie.'

THE REX GENE

The rex gene this was found to be of a recessive type. This means that, in order to be functional, one rex gene must be received from each parent. If only one parent has the gene, the coat of the offspring appears normal, but that individual still carries the gene and can pass it on to its future offspring.

If it is mated to a cat of the same genotype, there is a 25% chance of rex kittens, a 50% chance of rex carriers (called heterozygous or normal split for rex) and a 25% chance of kittens that carry no rex gene. There is no visual difference between the rex carrier and the non-rex cats. Only onward breeding can identify them.

increases the risk of infertility, and this too was a problem in the early years.

THE LOW POINT

By 1956, things were not going well for the developing breed from Cornwall. Becoming totally disillusioned by insufficient support and the growing financial burden of trying to maintain her cattery, Mrs Ennismore tried to sell many of her cats, but there were no takers prepared to pay realistic fees. As a result, Mrs Ennismore had most of the cats destroyed. These included both Kallibunker and Serena, which

Producing healthy kittens has always presented a challenge to breeders of the Cornish Rex.

The red tabby pattern is described as deeper rich red markings on a red ground.

The Devon Rex, shown here, bears a strong resemblance to its Cornish cousin.

this new 'type' would ever come to anything, let alone reach breed status. A few breeders were trying to work with the Rex, but not to the degree they could afford to invest in anything other than a small-scale programme.

During the 1950s, the cat fancy was a much smaller hobby and there were not the same opportunities to promote a breed as there are today. By 1957, it was thought that only one fertile Rex male existed—and he was in America! Fortunately, this proved not to be the case.

were put to sleep on 12 September 1956.

This was a sad day for the developing breed, and I am sure also for Mrs Ennismore, who must have been in a very depressed state by then. Part of the problem was that, by that time, the emerging breed had gained a reputation for its infertility.

The breed was not established, and many in the cat fancy were not convinced that

THE BREED SURVIVES

Mrs Ennismore had given to her vet a son of Kallibunker and Serena called Champagne Charlie. He was sent to Brian Sterling-Webb for breeding and was mated with Burmese and British Shorthairs. These outcrosses injected needed vigour into the breed, and in due course more

DEVON REX

In 1960, Mrs Beryl Cox of Buckfastleigh, Devon, discovered a rexed kitten, which she named Kirlee, within a litter of domestic shorthairs. Thinking that it would be of the same type as that discovered in Cornwall, she contacted Brian Sterling-Webb. Attempts to produce rex kittens by each type always failed, thus indicating that the two were quite separate mutations.

This subsequently was proved to be the case. Consequently, the name English Rex was dropped and the two varieties became separate breeds. While it is possible to create a double recessive rex, this is never recommended. There would be no benefit from doing this, especially from the perspective of the Cornish Rex coat and body type, the same being true of the Devon Rex body type.

The Russian Blue was used in outcrosses to help the survival of the Cornish Rex breed.

Outcrossing to the Siamese helped to strengthen the Cornish Rex's gene pool.

Rex were produced from these hybrids.

Other breeds, including the Russian Blue and Siamese, further strengthened the genetic pool and so helped ensure the breed's survival. Champagne Charlie was killed after two years of breeding as a consequence of a catfight in Sterling-Webb's cattery. Mrs Ennismore eventually ceased being a breeder in 1958.

THE BREED IN AMERICA

In 1957, Mrs Ennismore sent two cats to Mrs Blancheri in California. One, Pendennis Castle, proved infertile, but the second, Lamorna Cove, a blue female out of Poldhu and Millie Brim, had been mated to her father prior to export. She produced America's first litter. In it was a male called Marmaduke, who was acquired by Helen Weiss, and a female called Diamond Lil, who went to Peggy Galvin.

Diamond Lil was mated to a Siamese and produced kittens before she seemingly became infertile, as did Lamorna Cove. However, those hybrid kittens

Examples of the Burmese cat in chocolate and blue. This breed figured prominently in establishing the Cornish Rex.

The cream colour, a dilution of red, is seen in varying shades.

were to prove important in establishing the breed in America. Peggy Galvin and Ann Manley drafted the first American breed standard based on Diamond Lil, which the relatively small United Cat Federation accepted.

During the same period, Helen Weiss had attempted to obtain females from Mrs Ennismore, but to no avail. Three of the last four had been put to sleep. Consequently, Marmaduke was mated to his mother, but the whole litter died.

To ensure that his genes were perpetuated, Marmaduke was mated to a Siamese and again the outcross proved successful. The American Cornish Rex was thus largely developed from the offspring of Marmaduke and that of his sister.

However, while the Cornish Rex was being established in America, a German Rex also was being developed. It was decided to pair both types to see if they were compatible, which proved to be the case. As a consequence, the German Rex was used to provide outcross benefits to the Cornish. However, in due course, the German variety's lines were not sustained and faded into relative obscurity.

CORNISH RECOGNITION
The first major association to give the Rex official status was the Cat Fanciers Association (CFA) of America in 1964. Britain's Governing Council of the Cat Fancy (GCCF) did not grant status until 1967 but, from the outset, recognised that the Cornish Rex and Devon Rex were quite separate breeds. This did not happen with the CFA until 1979, though breeders had campaigned for it on obvious grounds. Prior to this, both British Rex breeds and the German Rex were lumped together as Rex cats. All other feline associations soon followed the lead of the GCCF.

While the world's major associations accepted all colours and patterns in the two main Rex breeds, the CFA was the exception. Not until 1985 were the Siamese and certain other patterns given recognition, even though these had been within the breed almost from its earliest development years in America.

The Cornish Rex has never gained top-ten popularity status, nor is it ever likely to. This should not be regarded as a

GERMAN REX
The German Rex was first identified about 1947 in a cat living in the ruins of Berlin in East Germany. She was a female given the name of Laemmchen by Dr Rose Scheuer-Karpin. One of her offspring, who became quite famous, was Marco Polo, who was displayed by Professor Letard at the 1960 Paris Cat Show. It was as a consequence of this exposure that awareness of the new breed spread and resulted in its being exported to America.

The German Rex never gained the same popularity as the Cornish, and many hobbyists assumed that it merged into the Cornish breed and thus into obscurity throughout mainland Europe. This is incorrect because the breed, though small in numbers, is recognised by the Federation Internationale Feline (FIFe) member associations throughout the world and by the Australian Cat Federation.

An intriguing chocolate and white Cornish Rex.

negative; it simply is a reflection of reality based on its (and most other breeds') record since it was first recognised. Surprisingly, it has never achieved registration figures comparable to the Devon Rex, which ranks quite high. In the CFA, these two Rex breeds enjoy almost the same popularity status.

There are major benefits to a breed's not becoming highly fashionable. It tends to be supported by dedicated owners and breeders who are hobbyists because of their love of the breed, ahead of any financial considerations. The downside is that breeders can be presented with genetic problems related to the small gene pool.

Head study showing many of the Cornish Rex's typical and desirable features: wedge-shaped head; high cheekbones; large, wide ears; and wrinkled whiskers.

CORNISH REX CAT

Of the two popular rexed cat breeds, the Cornish, apart from being older in respect to its establishment, is less extreme in its appearance than the Devon. Its coat is denser and less prone to bald patches. Though some examples may appear fairly dainty, the Cornish Rex is more muscular and heavier than might be thought.

While the majority of cat breeds have limitations placed on the number of colours or patterns in which they are officially accepted, the Cornish has no such restrictions. It is one of the few breeds that is, at least in theory, available in any colour or pattern as long as that colour or pattern is already seen in one or more recognised breeds.

BREED STANDARDS

When a new breed is developed, its pioneer breeders form a club and then draft a standard of excellence for the breed. This includes the colours and patterns that will be acceptable in that breed. The standard is then presented to one of the national registration associations and, hopefully, that association will adopt it.

The breed then can be called a recognised breed. The Cornish Rex enjoys breed recognition by

FORM AND FUNCTION

The unique build of the Cornish, together with its unusual coat, plays such an important role in determining most of its behaviour patterns. The Cornish is a slim cat with a body supported on long legs. This combination endows it with considerable athletic prowess. Such a build opens up many behavioural doors for the breed. It can move at high speed in both the vertical and horizontal planes, sometimes using its owner as a launching or landing site. Reaching the highest places in your home is very possible for the Cornish, whereas for many breeds these are in the 'look and forget it' category. As a consequence, it can get into all sorts of mischief that the sedate breeds would not, other than as kittens.

Its conformation also enables it to maintain its activity level for longer periods of time than can less athletically built cats: it is an economic fuel burner. It can, therefore, enthral you (or drive you mad, depending on your mood) for much longer periods than some breeds will.

WHAT ABOUT WHITE?

White is a popular colour for the Cornish Rex. It is seen in three varieties: blue-eyed, yellow-eyed (orange) and odd-eyed (one blue, one yellow). There are two points that should be mentioned with respect to the white colour. One is that it is associated with bilateral or unilateral deafness, more so in the blue-eyed than in the yellow-eyed.

The second point is that white is epistatic, meaning that it masks all colours. It does not remove the colours, which is why two white cats can pair and produce some coloured kittens. This assumes that neither of the pair are homozygous (pure-breeding) for the dominant white mutation that creates the colour white.

every cat registry in the world. Additionally, all registries apply the same flexibility in accepting all colours and patterns.

PRECISENESS OF A STANDARD

A cat's official standard can never be a definitive document because it would be impossible to describe exactly a cat breed in words. This being so, it is a somewhat vague description inasmuch as it contains many terms that describe relative states and that presume some knowledge on the part of the reader. The standard is therefore a general idealism against which a cat only can be assessed by experienced judges, breeders or enthusiasts of the given breed.

Interpretation of the standard by judges and breeders can result in a breed's changing over any span of time, as evidenced in the Persian and Siamese. You will, therefore, appreciate that while a standard is a crucially important document, its very looseness can of itself be the cause of change within a breed (and thus, it can be argued, generate problems as well as benefits to the breed).

All of this adds up to a simple fact. The beginner cannot hope to appreciate a standard unless they have some visual yardstick against which the words can be compared. That yardstick is the exhibits at a cat show. These cats will display what is considered to be a typical interpretation of the standard at that point in time.

The following description is not that of any single registry but was prepared after comparing those of three major associations.

Additional comments are included where these were thought to be helpful. The associations are the GCCF of Britain, the FIFe, which is international, and the CFA of America. This description should meet the needs of most owners. Potential breeders and exhibitors are advised to obtain the standard(s) of the breed from the association(s) with which their cats are registered.

The Cornish Rex in America is somewhat different from its European counterpart, but, as some European breeders are importing North American stock, the effect is that there is globally a wide range of types. Some Cornish Rex display a build that is quite lithe, whereas in Europe a somewhat stockier cat with a less Siamese-type head is preferred.

All of these meet the basics of the standards simply because the breed has a relatively short (and thus less detailed) standard in all countries.

BREED VARIANTS
Within the major registries, there are no specific breeds that are defined outcrosses to the Cornish Rex. This means that if the need to outcross is required, then any breed (or even moggie) can be used to this end. Outcrossing becomes a necessity from time to

White Cornish Rex, exhibiting blue eyes, which is one of the acceptable eye colorations in the white.

time within any breed that has a rather limited gene pool. This avoids the potential for a situation in which the general degree of relationships within the population may be considered to be too close. In other words, the degree of inbreeding is considered to be at risk of becoming unacceptably high, as it was in the earliest years of the Cornish Rex.

Outcrossing also is required when a new pattern or colour is to be introduced to a breed or when a breed-associated problem needs to be removed. The offspring of such a mating in this breed are called Cornish Rex variants. Because variants will not display the rexed coat (unless interbred, in which case a percentage will), they are obviously of little value to those other than breeders. They can be registered as Cornish Rex variants.

If you plan to own a Cornish Rex and would like a low-cost companion for it, you can help the breed by making this fact known to one of the Rex cat associations. Some of these variants can be stunningly beautiful felines. Variants that have the rexed coat will be somwhat more costly, but, as they cannot be exhibited until they are past the third generation from the outcross (unless exhibited in pet classes), they still represent sound, affordable purchases.

LAP CAT

If you are looking for a lap cat, the Cornish is as good as they come. The reason is logical, though not obvious. Densely furred and longhaired cats can quickly get too hot when sitting on your lap. Not so with the Cornish, which is quite happy on your lap, or wrapping itself around your neck, especially on those cooler nights. The breed's coat heat loss is such that the Cornish will often prefer to be under the bedclothes, whereas many other breeds are happier being on top of them, where it is cooler.

BREED DESCRIPTION

HEAD
When viewed from the front, the head has the appearance of a wedge, but one in which the high cheekbones are gently rounded. In

Head study of an American Cornish Rex, in profile.

America, where the breed is rather different from that in Europe and elsewhere, the CFA describes the head as egg-shaped, both in frontal and profile views.

In profile, the skull is flat and makes a slight curving change of direction at the forehead before continuing in a straight line to the tip of the nose. In America, the nose is preferred to be of the high-bridge Roman type (displaying a convex curve). There is no stop (a definite dip where the forehead meets the nose). The muzzle narrows to a rounded, strong chin. The length of the head is about one-third longer than the maximum width of the head. The GCCF standard calls for crinkled whiskers, but of good length. In reality, many of the European-type Cornish display normal whiskers, reflecting the influence of the outcrosses to domestic moggies.

EYES

In Europe, the eyes are oval-shaped and of medium size; in America, they are medium to large. The shape of the face, which can make similar sizes look rather different, influences apparent eye size in any cat breed. Likewise, the colour of the facial fur and the eyes also will make the eyes a more, or less, noticeable feature. The eyes should be set a full eye's width apart.

EYE COLOUR

Any eye colour is acceptable, though the CFA adds that it should be appropriate to the coat colour. This means that colour-point (Si-Rex) individuals will have blue eyes, and white cats will have blue, yellow or one eye in each of these colours (called odd-eyed white). Other eye colours in cats are gold, copper, orange, green and aquamarine.

EARS

The ears are large, wide at their basal openings, set high on the head and tapering to rounded tips. Their outer edges are relatively straight.

BODY

This is not a large breed, its slender body being of medium size and length, and covered with solid muscle. In America, the standard calls for a torso of long length while the hips should be muscular and some-what heavy compared to the rest of the body.

The Whippet-like appearance of this breed, especially in America, derives from its arched back coupled with a tucked-up abdomen when in a normal pose, plus a Whippet-like tail. This is much less evident in stock of British and European ancestry and reflects the greater influence of the Siamese on the breed in America.

LEGS
The legs should be long, with the hindlegs being longer than the front legs. The bone is strong but has a delicate look to it. The paws are small and oval.

TAIL
The tail should be long, slender and flexible, and should taper to a rounded tip. It should be well covered with wavy fur.

COAT
Plush, short and of a silky texture, the coat lacks guard hairs. How-ever, it must still be quite dense. The coat must display curls, Marcel waves or ripples. These should cover the entire body, tail and chin.

FAULTS
For exhibition purposes, faults are divided into two broad categories: those that apply to all breeds and those that are breed-specific. Here we are concerned only with breed-specific faults, which are shaggy or long coats, coarse coats and/or those displaying guard hairs, coats that have bare

Overall, the body should be medium-sized and slender, with a long slender tail. This striking coloration is the chocolate tortie smoke.

CORNISH REX SELF-COLOURS*

not including white

COLOUR	DESCRIPTION
Black	A popular colour, it ideally should be a coal black free from rustiness, which may be created by its genotype or by the bleaching action of sunlight.
Blue	Blue is very variable in its shade from dark to light. It is more of a grey-blue, or slate, than a true blue. It is a popular colour created by a mutation that dilutes black.
Chocolate	This is a medium to dark chocolate created by a mutation that degrades black to brown. It is not a commonly seen colour, but one that is becoming more so.
Lilac	Also called lavender or platinum in America, it is a dove-grey, created by the dilution of chocolate.
Cinnamon	A somewhat more reddish light brown than chocolate, cinnamon is created by a second mutation found at the black pigment locus.
Fawn	A rosy beige or pinkish-mushroom, fawn is created by the dilution of cinnamon.
Caramel	One of the latest colours, caramel is a pale, bluish fawn. It is created by a mutation that works only on the dilute colours, which is called the dilute modifier. Caramel results from the mutation working on the blue, lilac or fawn.
Apricot	When the dilute modifier works on cream, the result is an intense pinkish-cream called apricot.
Red	Red should be a very intense, rich brick colour in exhibition cats. It is quite different from the ginger seen in typical moggies. Its intensity is the result of rufous polygenes' working on the red mutation, which is a sex-linked colour in cats.
Cream	The dilution of red, cream is quite a variable colour that can be light to medium cream or buff depending on the rufous polygenic background of the red.

patches, lack of waves in the coat, small ears, low-set ears, head too long or broad, cobby body and lack of good musculature.

COLOURS AND PATTERNS

With a potential range that runs into over a thousand combinations, it will be appreciated that all of these cannot be discussed. Some colours and patterns are very popular. Others are rarely, if ever, seen.

SELF-COLOURS

This term means the entire cat is of the given colour. Ideally, the colour should be sound down to the roots and be free of shading and white hairs. Shading is where there are areas that are darker than others. There are presently ten colours—black, blue, chocolate, lilac, cinnamon, fawn, caramel, apricot, red and cream— plus white, seen in domestic breeds.

PATTERNS

Of the many potential coat patterns, a few are very popular, but most are relatively unknown to the potential owner not presently well acquainted with the cat fancy.

Some patterns are strongly associated with certain breeds such that, even when they are seen in other breeds, they still are referred to under the name of the breed in which they first

COAT PATTERNS	
Agouti	Pigments band the hair, named after the rodent that possesses this pattern.
Non-agouti	Coat colour exhibits a self-colour or carries two or more colours.
Shell	Darker colour on tips of the hair; lower portion lighter in colour.
Shaded	Darker colour extends further than the tip, as in the shell.
Bi-colour	Solid colour with white pattern.

appeared—the Siamese is possibly the best example. The patterns may be seen in each of the colours, or in certain of them, and two or even three patterns can be combined.

The following is a brief overview of most patterns, some of which you might have to search a long while to find in the Cornish Rex. All are included for completeness and in order that the beginner is aware of the patterns and their official names.

Tabby: There are four varieties of the tabby, and they essentially differ in the body markings. On the head, all carry the 'M' or scarab mark. The legs and tail are ringed with bands, which extend onto the chest.

The mackerel tabby is distinguished by the numerous stripes

that run vertically down the body sides. It is often referred to in America as the tiger tabby. The classic or blotched tabby features a large oyster-shaped blotch on each flank, which is encircled with unbroken bands. Although the mackerel pattern is the older, it is the classic pattern that has always dominated the cat fancy.

The spotted tabby has body spots and rosettes of various sizes, which should not be arranged in a vertical (mackerel) manner. The ticked tabby has a coat in which the dark and lighter banded hairs overlap each other such as to produce a ticked effect, called agouti. The tabby patterns are always popular.

Bi-colour: In this pattern, any of the self-colours are combined

TABBY COLOURS

COLOUR	DESCRIPTION	EYE COLOUR
BROWN	Tawny sable ground with dense black markings.	ORANGE/COPPER
BLUE	Pale blue ground with darker blue markings.	ORANGE/COPPER
CHOCOLATE	Bronze ground with chocolate brown markings.	HAZEL OR COPPER
LILAC	Beige ground with lilac markings.	HAZEL OR COPPER
RED	Red ground with deeper rich red markings.	ORANGE/COPPER
SILVER	Silver ground with dense black markings.	GREEN OR HAZEL

COLOURPOINT

SOLID POINT COLOURS

POINT COLOUR	BODY COLOUR
SEAL BROWN	Beige shading to creamy white.
BLUE	Bluish white shading to white.
CHOCOLATE	Ivory shading to white.
LILAC	Magnolia white shading to white.
RED	Apricot shading to white.
CREAM	Lighter cream shading to white.

TORTIE POINT COLOURS

POINT COLOUR	BODY COLOUR
SEAL BROKEN WITH SHADES OF RED	Toning cream.
BLUE-CREAM BLUE BROKEN WITH SHADES OF CREAM	Glacial to creamy white.
CHOCOLATE BROKEN WITH SHADES OF RED	Ivory to apricot white.
LILAC-CREAM LILAC BROKEN WITH SHADES OF CREAM	Magnolia to creamy.

TABBY POINT COLOURS

The tabby is restricted to the points. The colours are seal, blue, chocolate, lilac, red and cream.

TORTIE TABBY POINT COLOURS

Both the tortie and the tabby elements must be present, though the extent and distribution of these are not important. The colours are seal, blue-cream, chocolate and lilac-cream.

with white. Although the extent and placement of white is of importance in a show cat, it is not directly under the breeder's control, so there is a random aspect to it. This means that the amount and placement of the white are such that these cats are always uniquely marked.

Bi-colour is a very popular pattern. When the colour is restricted to the head, legs and tail, it is called 'van' after the Turkish Van breed.

Tipped Patterns: There are three grades of tipped patterns in cats. These are named according to the extent of the pigment in each hair shaft. If the hairs are pigmented two-thirds of their length from the tip, this is called smoke. In the Cornish, this is very popular.

If the pigment extends down one-third of the hair shaft, this is called shaded; if only the tips are pigmented, this is called chinchilla. The non-tipped part of the hair should be as near to white as possible. If the shaded pattern is seen in red, this is called shaded cameo, while the

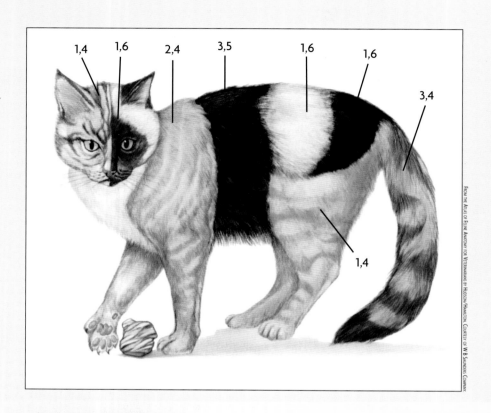

1,4   1,6   2,4   3,5   1,6   1,6   3,4   1,4

FROM THE ATLAS OF FELINE ANATOMY FOR VETERINARIANS BY HUDSON/HAMILTON, COURTESY OF W B SAUNDERS COMPANY

PARTICOLOURED CAT

Not a new breed of feline, this 'particoloured cat' illustrates the many possibilities of the feline coat. Since cats come in three basic hair lengths, short, long and rex, all three coat lengths are illustrated here. Additionally, different coat patterns, such as mackerel tabby, Abyssinian and self-coloured, are depicted to demonstrate the differences.

1–3   COAT TYPES
  1 Shorthair coat
  2 Rex coat
  3 Longhair coat

4–6   COAT COLOUR PATTERNS
  4 Mackerel (tabby)
  5 Abyssinian
  6 Self-coloured

SKIN AND HAIRCOAT OF CATS

Schematic illustration of histologic layers of the integument skin.

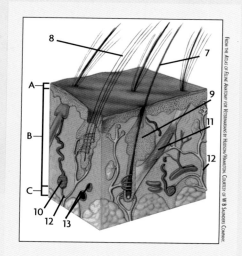

A Epidermis
B Dermis
C Subcutis

7 Primary hair
8 Secondary hairs
9 Area of sebaceous gland
10 Apocrine sweat gland
11 M arrector pili
12 Nerve fibre
13 Cutaneous vessels
14 Tactile hair
15 Fibrous capsule
16 Venous sinus
17 Sensory nerve fibres
18 External root sheath
19 Hair papilla

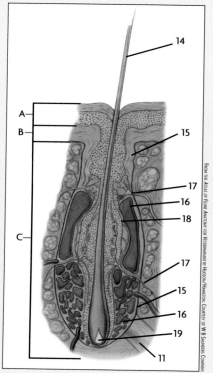

Schematic illustration of a tactile hair (whisker).

chinchilla becomes the shell cameo.

Colourpoint: This pattern is commonly known as Siamese. The term colourpoint is used in breeds to denote that it is the pattern of the Siamese that has been transferred to the given breed. Genetically, it is called the Siamese colour restriction. It is one of a series of mutations that go from full colour to albino.

In this pattern the face, ears, legs and tail are a darker colour than that of the rest of the body. In the Cornish Rex, the term Si-Rex is still in use, including within the GCCF. As it is suggestive of a Siamese x Cornish Rex hybrid, it is perhaps a less

desirable term than colourpoint.

Burmese: Genetically called the Burmese colour restriction, it is in the same series as the Siamese. In this pattern, there is far less contrast between the points and the body colours, with the two gently merging, as compared to the sharp contrast required in the Siamese (colour-point). The term Burmese is used for this pattern when seen in the Cornish Rex.

Tonkinese: When a cat inherits a colourpoint gene from one parent and a Burmese restriction from another, neither gene is able to express itself fully. The result is an appearance midway between the two types. This is the

The tortoiseshell and white Cornish Rex would be called a calico in America. This Rex is a female, of course.

basis of the breed called the Tonkinese. When the pattern is seen in other breeds, it is usually called mink. In the GCCF, this pattern is referred to as being 'darker points.'

Tortoiseshell: This very old pattern, commonly called tortie, is unusual because it is sex-linked. In it, two colours are able to express themselves visually. One is black and the other is red in various shades. In Britain, it is preferred that the colours are evenly intermingled, whereas in America, they should appear as distinct patches of black and red. In the early years of the cat fancy in Britain, distinct patches of colour were the ideal. White can be combined with the pattern to form the tortie and white—known as calico in America.

Occasionally tortie males are produced, though they are invariably sterile. Poldhu, one of the first Cornish Rex, was an exception. In the statistics of the CFA over a 39-year period, just 14 of 2178 Cornish Rex torties were male. It is because of the torties produced by females that most red cats are males, usually in the ratio of 2:1.

Sex linkage is simple in its working. A male cat has one X and one Y chromosome in his reproductive cells. The shorter Y appears to be devoted to matters of gender. The female has two X chromosomes.

The colour red is created by a dominant mutation on the X chromosome and is designated O for orange. Its alternate form (normal wild-type) acts as a recessive to this and results in the base colour (black, blue, chocolate or whatever) and is designated as o (non-red). A male can be XOY (red) or XoY (non-red). A female can be XOXO (red), XoXo (non-red) or XOXo (tortie heterozygote).

The uniqueness of the heterozygous combination lies in the fact that the red can express itself in the coat because it is a dominant mutation that masks any other colours. However, it is not able to mask the colours in other areas of the coat, which can thus manifest themselves and display whatever the base colour is. If the dilute genes are present in both parents, these will produce the popular blue-cream variety.

Kittens of different colours and patterns can appear in the same litter. Among this white mum's brood are a tortie and white (centre) and red and white.

The irresistible appeal of a wide-eyed kitten is undeniable, but you must use your head, not just your heart, in deciding to add a Cornish Rex to your home.

Purchasing a —————
CORNISH REX CAT

Before the decision to purchase a Cornish Rex is made, careful consideration should be given to the implications and responsibilities of cat ownership. If more owners would do this, there would be far fewer half-starved pets roaming our streets or having to live in local animal-rescue centres.

OWNER RESPONSIBILITY

The initial cost of a Cornish Rex represents only a fraction of its lifetime's cost. The first question is, 'Can you afford one?' The kitten needs vaccinations to protect it against various diseases. Boosters are then required every year. Cat food is more costly than that for dogs. There is also the cost of cat litter every week. Periodic vet checks and treatment for illness or accidents must be allowed for. When holidays are taken, you may need to board the pet at a cattery.

From the outset, there will be additional costs apart from that of the kitten. It will need a basket, carrying box, feeding and grooming utensils, scratching post, a few toys and maybe a collar. If you have any doubts at

THE PURCHASING PROCESS

Never rush into the purchase of a companion that is to be given the freedom of your home and will become an integral part of your life. A pure-bred cat may live 20 or more years. This is a long time. It is very prudent to take all those steps that will minimise the chances of your ever regretting the choice you make. Once you have decided on the sex, age, reason for purchase (pet, show or breeding) and desired colour pattern, proceed cautiously, heeding all of the advice given here. By following a planned process of selection, you also will gain much useful information.

all about being able to supply all of these needs, it is best not to obtain a cat.

Other matters also need careful thought. If you are planning to have a family, will your love for the Cornish Rex be compromised once a baby arrives? Cats are generally not a problem with family newcomers, providing they are not ignored or treated as being a threat to the baby. Never purchase a kitten for a child unless you want one yourself. If you are elderly, it is only fair to consider what would happen to your cherished pet if it were to outlive you or if you were to become hospitalised for long periods.

It is most unfortunate that many people rush into the purchase of cats on impulse. They then find they cannot cope if problems, and extra costs, ensue. Some lose interest in the pet once it matures past its cute kitten stage. The evidence of these realities is easily seen in the growing number of cats abandoned or taken to animal shelters every year. Invariably their owners will make feeble excuses for why the cat cannot be kept. But the bottom line is they did not stop to consider at the outset what responsible ownership entailed.

The Cornish Rex is an active cat that overflows with the joys of life. If you are the sort of person who wants to interact with your feline companion, you will be delighted with this breed. If you

DOCUMENTATION

When you take delivery of your kitten, certain paperwork should come with it:

1. Three- to five-generation pedigree.
2. Breeder-signed registration application form or change of owner registration form. This assumes the breeder has registered stock. If he has not, the kitten cannot be registered at a later date. It is worth less than the kitten with registration paperwork. You are not recommended to purchase a kitten from unregistered parents.
3. Certificates of health, vaccination and neutering, if this has been effected. Ideally, it is desirable that the kitten's parents have been tested negative for major diseases. Additionally, the breeder should know the blood group of your kitten. This may be of importance at a later date.
4. Details of worming or other treatments attended.
5. Diet sheet, feeding timetable and brand names of food items used. This diet should be maintained for at least ten days while the kitten adjusts to the trauma of moving home.
6. Signed receipt for monies paid.
7. Signed copy of any guarantees. Not all breeders give a guarantee on the reasonable grounds that once the kitten leaves the breeder's care, its onward well-being is no longer under his control.

are very house-proud, the sort who does not like things disturbed, then forget a Cornish. Indeed, such people should forget any cat breed and think in terms of fishkeeping.

The Cornish loves to disturb things and be involved in everything. This enables it to learn how things can be done even better. Knocking items from shelves requires much practice and skill to perfect to art status! Climbing curtains and leaping across the room can be done in a clumsy or skilful manner—it all comes down to the extent of regular practice.

Everything about the Cornish is such that it is a breed that needs lots of attention and consid-

No matter whether you choose a kitten or an adult cat, all children in the family must treat the new pet with care and respect.

eration. This, in turn, will pay handsome dividends in its patterns of behaviour. You will then join all other Cornish owners who believe that this really is a breed that is different from any other.

KITTEN OR ADULT?

Most potential owners normally want a kitten because it is so cute, cuddly and playful. A kitten is easily trained and has not yet developed bad habits, which the older Cornish may have done. This said, if you plan to breed or exhibit, there are advantages in obtaining a young adult. Other potential owners, such as the

TAKING KITTY HOME

Arrange collection of the kitten as early in the day as possible. If a long journey is involved, be sure to take a few breaks so kitty does not suffer from travel sickness. Do not make stops to show the kitten to friends; this represents an health hazard. Once home, offer the kitten a drink, then allow it to sleep if it so requires. Children must be educated to handle a kitten gently, never to tease it and to respect its sleeping privacy. Until it is litter-trained, it should be restricted to the kitchen or another room with an easy-to-clean floor surface.

elderly, may benefit by avoiding the demanding needs of a young kitten. In both of these instances, a good age is when the youngster is 9–15 months old. Even a fully-mature Cornish Rex may prove an excellent choice for some owners.

Kittens should not be obtained under 12 weeks old, though 14–16 weeks is better. No reputable breeder will sell them younger than this. Less caring breeders will let them go to new homes as young as eight weeks of age. Such juveniles will barely have been weaned. They will not have developed the needed resistance to major diseases. They are more likely to become stressed by the premature removal from their mother and siblings. Their vaccinations will not be fully effective. These factors will dramatically increase the risk of immediate problems.

ADOPTING AN ADULT

Some owners may benefit by adopting an adult cat. They can avoid the demanding needs of a young kitten and enjoy the advantages of a well-trained adult, making grooming an easier task. Breeders and exhibitors can also benefit from purchasing an older cat because it is easier to assess the quality. Sometimes, though, older cats can have bad habits that are hard to break. So, if you are thinking about obtaining an older cat, it is important to thoroughly investigate possible behavioural and health problems.

SEX & COLOUR PATTERN

If it is to be purely a pet, the Cornish's gender is unimportant. Both are delightful. Males are usually larger, bolder and more outgoing. Females tend to be more discerning about which humans they like. However, each Cornish Rex is an individual. Its character and health, more than its sex, should be the basis of selection. Again, the sex is unimportant for the potential exhibitor. It is not even necessary for the cat to be sexually 'entire.' Classes for neuters are featured in shows.

Those with breeding aspirations are advised to obtain only females. All pet owners should regard neutering (males) and spaying (females) as obligatory. Today this can be effected at any age after eight weeks.

The colour pattern is a matter

Not every colour is numerous; therefore, all colours will not be readily available. This may affect your choice, but remember that overall health and soundness are more important qualities than colour.

While human toys may look fun to a curious kitty, they are not as safe. Provide your Cornish Rex with a variety of sturdy cat toys that encourage active play, which will be sure to hold its interest.

of personal preference. It should never be placed ahead of health and character. Some colours and patterns will be more readily available than others. The more popular varieties may be less costly than the rarer ones. This would generally not apply to prospective breeding or exhibition individuals, where type quality will be as important as colour or pattern.

LOOK BEFORE YOU LEAP

It is important you meet as many Cornish Rex breeders and kittens as you can. This gives you a good mental picture of what an healthy typical example should look like and cost for the quality and colour you want. Normally, you will get what you pay for. If you look for the cheapest kitten, there will be a sound reason why it is the cheapest!

The best place to start your search is a cat show. At large cat shows, most of the colour varieties will be on display. Purchase the show catalogue. It lists all of the exhibitors and their addresses. You can see if any live in your immediate locality. Whenever possible, it is best to purchase locally so you can visit the home of the breeder. Some breeders will insist you do so in order to be satisfied that you will make a good owner.

Shows and breeders are advertised in the various cat magazines available from newsagents. You also can contact a major cat registry, which will supply a list of national and regional clubs, which are usually able to supply breeder lists. When visiting a breeder, always make an appointment. Try to visit no more than one cattery a day. This reduces the risk of your transporting pathogens (disease-causing organisms) from one establishment to the next. Selecting a good breeder is a case of noting the environment in which the cats are kept, the attitude of the owner to you and their cats and how friendly and healthy the kittens look. It is vital that the chosen kitty has an outgoing personality. It must not appear timid or very shy. This indicates a lack of breeder sociali-sation or a genetic weakness in its temperament. Either way, it is not a kitten that you should select.

CHOOSING A KITTEN

If you choose the breeder wisely, and especially if a friend recommends him, this will greatly reduce the risk of any problems related to your making a poor choice. However, a little knowledge on what to look for will not go amiss. Observe the kittens from a distance to ensure that none is unduly lethargic, which is never a good sign. If any kitten displays signs of illness, this should bring to an end any further thoughts of purchase from

AN HEALTHY KITTEN

Closely inspect any kitten before making a final decision. Keep in mind the following points:

Eyes and nose: Clean and clear with no signs of discharge.
Ears: Fresh-smelling and erect.
Coat: Healthy, not dull or dry.
Anal region: Clean with no staining of the fur.
Feet: Four toes on each foot, plus a dewclaw on the inside of each front leg.
Teeth: Correct bite.

There should be no signs of parasites. A potbelly may indicate worms.

that source. A reputable breeder would not allow a sickly kitten to remain within its litter.

It is always advisable to select a kitten that shows particular interest in you. Cornish Rex are very discerning. If both of you are drawn to each other, this will greatly enhance the bonding essential for a strong relationship.

Once a particular kitten has been selected, it should be given a close physical inspection. The eyes and nose must show no signs of weeping or discharge. The ears will be erect and fresh-smelling. The coat should look healthy, never dry and dull. There must be no signs of parasites in the fur. There will be no bodily swellings or abrasions. Lift the tail and inspect the anal region. This must be clean with no indication of congealed faecal matter. Any staining of the fur indicates current or recent diarrhoea.

The kitten must not display a potbelly. This may indicate worms or other internal disorders. Check the teeth to be sure of a correct bite. Bear in mind that the jawbones do not develop at the same rate. Minor imperfections may correct themselves (they may also get worse), but major faults will not. Inspect the feet to see there are four toes on each, plus a dewclaw on the inside of each front leg.

With respect to colour, there is no link between this and health other than deafness in certain white varieties. Any faults in the colour or its placement will only be of importance in breeding and/or exhibition individuals. The potential breeder/exhibitor should obtain a copy of the official breed standard so that he is *au fait* with all colour, pattern and bodily faults of the breed.

CAT LITTER

The litter that is used in cat boxes can be very variable, and, in many cases, cats reject the use of a cat box because of the litter. Certainly, if your cat rejects the use of the cat box, you should try different litters. You can start with the litters available at your local pet shop, then you can try sand, dirt, cedar shavings or whatever will appeal to your cat. Several cat owners grow clover in trays and their cats seem to prefer that. However, the trays are kept outdoors and the cats may simply be marking the clover tray rather than using them for elimination purposes.

HOMEMADE TOYS

Cats love to play and pet shops have many cat toys to choose from. Sometimes, however, people give their cats homemade toys. These can be harmful to your cat, as they could have pieces that could break off and be swallowed. Only give your pet toys from the pet shop that have been proven safe for cats.

Your local pet shop will carry a variety of litter boxes and trays from which you can select the one best suited to your needs.

There are many kinds of scratching posts from which you may choose a post that will interest your Cornish Rex.

Cat carriers are a necessity of cat ownership, though no cat welcomes the opportunity of being carted about in a crate. Nonetheless, the carrier is the only safe option for transport.

Double-bowl feeders are very convenient for feeding your cat. Go to your pet shop to purchase top-quality feeders, which should come in a variety of colours, styles and sizes.

There is nothing glamorous about purchasing a litter box, yet cat owners have few options in this regard. Consult your local pet shop to see a selection of boxes. Some cats do not accept a covered box, while others welcome the 'privacy.'

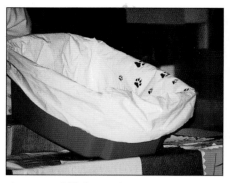

Liners are available for most litter trays to assist in keeping them clean and more manageable.

Purchasing a scratching post is a smart option for the cat owner. It's best to purchase a sturdy, well-made post that will last your cat years of utility.

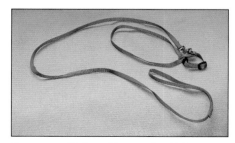

If you are considering walking your Cornish Rex, you must have a lead that is suitable for a cat.

With such a variety of cat toys available, it can be as entertaining for you to watch your Cornish Rex with his toys as it is for the cat to play with them!

KITTY SHOPPING SPREE

Certain accessories should be regarded as obligatory and obtained before the kitten arrives at your home.

SCRATCHING POST

This will save the furniture from being abused! There are many models, some being simple posts, while others are combined with play stations and sleeping quarters, which are the best for keeping a cat's interest.

LITTER BOX(ES)

Some are open trays; others are domed to provide extra privacy. Some have special bases in which odour removers are fitted.

CAT LITTER

There are numerous types on the market, each offering advantages and drawbacks. Avoid the low-cost types that contain a lot of dangerous dust. Use those that are fully biodegradable.

FOOD/WATER DISHES

Polished metal has the longest wear life. Earthenware is less costly than metal and superior to the plastic types.

GROOMING TOOLS

Among the tools needed are a good-quality bristle brush, a fine-toothed comb, nail trimmers and a soft chamois leather.

CAT COLLAR AND/OR HARNESS

Select an elasticised collar. Be sure that a name and address disc or barrel is fitted to this. An harness must be a snug but comfortable fit if it is to be effective.

CARRYING BOX

This is essential for transporting the cat to the vet or other places, as well as for home restriction when needed. Be sure that it is large enough to accommodate a fully-grown Cornish, not just a kitten. The choice is between collapsible models, soft plastic types and, the best choice, those made of wood or fibreglass.

This scratching post, with a perch on top, gives cats the opportunity to scratch, jump and climb...all favourite feline activities!

CORNISH REX CAT

For a kitten, its human environment holds many dangers. Its owner must protect it from these until it becomes agile and wiser. The following dangers lurk in typical households. Always check whether there are additional hazards in your home. The most important decision you need to make from the outset is whether or not the kitten is to be given outdoor liberty.

HOW MUCH FREEDOM?

More than at any time in the past, the question of how much freedom a cat should be given is the subject of heated debate. It is a very subjective matter. Here the more pertinent points are given so you can relate these to your home environment. This, to a very large degree, should influence your decision.

Cats living in or close to an urban area are at the highest safety risk. The amount of traffic is such that death from road accidents is a major concern. In such environments, there are high dog populations, some of which are feral. Injury or death from dog attacks is therefore another major source of danger to a feline.

Urban cat populations are also extremely high. Far too many cats are living a virtually feral existence. These are tough, street-wise cats that often carry fleas and other parasites that are vectors of disease. Some will be carriers of, or infected with, feline leukaemia and other deadly diseases.

The typical feline family pet can be badly injured if it becomes engaged in fights with these roaming bullies. Furthermore, their very presence in and around a gentle cat's garden can cause the pet severe stress. This can make it fearful of stepping outside its home. In

THE GARAGE AND SHED

These two buildings are very dangerous to a kitten. Sharp and heavy tools, nails, glass jars, garden weed killers and open tins of paint are but a sampling of the items that the average family uses or stores in these. A kitten may clamber into the engine compartment of a vehicle, which could be fatal if the owner happened to start the engine before the kitten had removed itself. Always know where the kitten is.

BE ONE JUMP AHEAD

Seemingly innocuous things, such as doors, can become life-threatening should they suddenly slam shut on a kitten due to a strong draught. When windows and external doors are open, be sure internal doors are secured with a doorstop. At all times, be one jump ahead of a kitten in terms of identifying dangerous situations.

some instances, it may cause the pet to actually leave its home.

Sadly, if these risks are not enough, there is no shortage of people who will steal a pedigreed cat, the more so if it is friendly. Add to this the number of abusive people who do not like cats roaming into their gardens, and the scenario is not good. Finally, free-roaming cats also take an heavy toll on local bird and wildlife populations.

Taking these various facts into account, the urban cat is best kept indoors. It can enjoy the benefit of the outdoors if supplied with a roomy aviary-type exercise pen. Some cats can be trained to walk on a lead. This allows outdoor enjoyment, even if this is restricted to the garden. When walking your cat in public places, use only an harness. This is much safer than a collar.

In contrast to urban situations, the cat living in a rural environ-

ment is far safer, the more so if there are no immediate neighbours or busy roads. Even so, it is wise to restrict the cat's outdoor freedom to daylight hours. During the night, it is more likely to get run over or to threaten local wildlife.

Those living between the extremes of isolated areas and busy urban environments should consider the local risk factor. Generally, it is best to keep the cat indoors but to provide an outdoor exercise pen.

THE TRAVELLING CAT

Whenever your cat needs to be taken on a car journey, never let it travel loose in the vehicle, which is illegal. It must always be in its carrying box. If a cat were to go under the clutch or brake pedal when the car was moving, this would be dangerous to all occupants. A cat might also spring from one seat to another, which might distract the driver. This could have disastrous results.

Never leave a cat alone in a car on an hot day. The temperature can rise dramatically to the point that the cat is unable to breathe. It could die of heat stroke. Always leave a window partially open when you are in the car with your cat on an hot day, so the cat can stay cool in its carrier.

Many families own more than one cat peacefully, but, in multi-cat households, introductions must be made carefully so that no unexpected incidents occur.

HOUSEHOLD DANGERS

Within its home, a kitten is best viewed as an accident waiting to happen! The most dangerous room is the kitchen. Hot electric hobs, naked flames from gas rings, boiling pans of food or water and sinks full of water are obvious hazards. An iron left on its board with the cable trailing to the floor is an invitation to a kitten to jump up—with potentially fatal consequences. Washing machines or spin dryers with warm clothes in them, and their doors open, are inviting places to nap. Always check the kitty isn't inside if the door has been left open. Cupboards containing poisonous or other dangerous substances should always be kept securely closed.

In the living room, the normal dangers are aquariums without hoods, unguarded fires, electric bar heaters, poisonous indoor plants, trailing electrical leads and ornaments that may be knocked over by a mischievous kitty. Toilets can be fatal to an over-curious kitten. The same is true of a bath containing water. Balconies should be safeguarded to remove the potential for the kitten to slip and fall.

garden containing a pond, the kitten must be under constant supervision. Cherished ornaments should be placed out of reach of the kitten, as much for their safety as to any danger they may present to the kitty. It's not always the direct danger of something that can be the problem. If an ornament or similar item crashes to the floor, this can startle the kitten into a panicked departure! The kitten could then fall from a shelf in its haste. Of course, all safety measures are equally as important for adult cats.

DANGEROUS DISINFECTANTS

Although owners should disinfect the litter box regularly to prevent disease and illness, some household disinfectants can be harmful to cats. Pine-oil-based cleaners are toxic to cats. DO NOT use them. Products containing Phenol should also be avoided. Bleach is a good disinfectant to use; however, be sure to rinse the litter box thoroughly and air it out to get rid of any fumes.

OTHER DANGERS

Other potential dangers are when electric tools are left lying about and connected to power outlets—even worse if they are left on, as with bench saws. If the kitten is given freedom to exercise in a

Your Cornish Rex wants to be part of everything but, in his investigations, may find itself in some precarious positions. Do your best to create a harm-free environment for your cat.

Feeding Your
CORNISH REX CAT

Today, the feeding of cats has been reduced to its most simple level with the availability of many scientifically prepared commercial diets. However, this fact can result in owners' becoming casual in their approach to the subject. While the main object of a given diet is to provide the ingredients that promote healthy growth and maximum immunity to disease, it also fulfils an important secondary role.

A proper diet must maintain in the cat a psychological feeling of well-being that avoids nutritionally related stress problems or syndromes. By ensuring that the diet is balanced, of good variety and never monotonous, these dual roles will be achieved. This approach will also avoid the situation of the cat's becoming a finicky eater.

BALANCE AND VARIETY
A balanced diet means one that contains all of the major ingredients—protein, fats, carbohydrates, vitamins and minerals—in the ratios needed to ensure maximum growth and health. Variety means

By allowing cats to feed together, it will be hard to determine if each one is getting its proper share.

supplying foods in a range of forms that will maintain and stimulate the cat's interest in its meals. Commercially formulated foods come in three levels of moisture: low (dried foods), semi-moist and moist (tinned foods).

Generally, the low and moist forms are the most popular. Dried cat foods have the advantage that they can be left in the cat dish for longer periods of time than tinned foods. They are ideal for supplying on a free-choice basis. Like the tinned varieties, they come in a wide range of popular flavours.

In order to meet the specific needs of a kitten, there are specially formulated foods available. These contain the higher protein levels needed by a growing kitten. As it grows, the kitten can be weaned slowly onto the adult types. There are also special brands available from vets for any kitten or cat that may have a dietary problem as well as special diets for the older cat. These may need lower ratios of certain ingredients, such as proteins and sodium, so as to reduce the workload of the liver.

Flavours should be rotated so that interest in meals is maintained. This also encourages familiarity with different tastes. Naturally, Cornish Rex will display a greater liking for certain flavours and brands than for others.

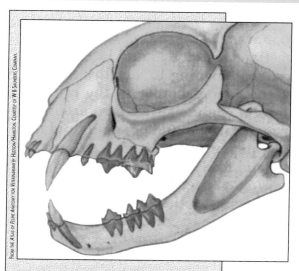

FROM THE ATLAS OF FELINE ANATOMY FOR VETERINARIANS BY HUDSON/HAMILTON, COURTESY OF W B SAUNDERS COMPANY.

MEET THE MEAT-EATERS
Since cats are carnivorous, their teeth are designed to bite and cut. Except for crunching dried foods, cats do very little chewing. They have the fewest teeth of any common domestic mammal—typically 30 (although there are some variations). The canine teeth usually are more developed than the incisors.

FRESH FOODS
To add greater variety and interest, there are many fresh foods that Cornish Rex enjoy. Some will be very helpful in cleaning the teeth and exercising the jaw muscles. All have the benefit of providing different textures and smells that help stimulate the palate. Feed these foods two or three times a week as treats or occasionally as special meals.

EAT YOUR HAIRBALLS AWAY
Food companies have developed formulas containing a wholesome fibre blend that moves ingested hair through the cat's digestive tract, thus minimising the occurrence of hairballs. Tests show that feeding these formulas moved 80% more hair through the digestive tract, meaning fewer hairballs!

Cooked poultry, including the skin but minus the bones, is usually a favourite, as is quality raw or cooked mincemeat. Cooked beef on the bone gives the cat something to enjoy. Cooked white fish, as well as tinned tuna or sardines, are examples of ocean delights. Never feed raw fish; this can prove dangerous, even fatal. Although cats rarely enjoy items such as rice, pasta or cooked vegetables, these can nonetheless be finely chopped and mixed with meats or fish. Some Cornish Rex may develop a taste for them. Various cheeses and scrambled or boiled eggs will often be appreciated—but never give raw eggs.

If the diet is balanced and varied, the addition of vitamin and mineral supplements is unnecessary and can actually prove dangerous. While certain of these compounds are released from the body if in excess, others are not. They are stored and can adversely affect efficient metabolism. If a cat shows loss of condition and disinterest in its food, discuss its diet with a vet.

HOW MUCH TO FEED
Food intake is influenced by many factors. These are the cat's age, activity level, the ambient temperature (more is eaten in the colder months), the cat's breeding state (rearing kittens) and the quality of the food. Always follow the breeder's recommendations on diet until your kitten has settled into your home. Thereafter, the needed quantity will increase as the kitten gets older, until full maturity at about two to three years of age.

As a basic guide, a four-month-old kitten will require four meals a day. At six months of age, one meal can be dropped. By twelve months of age, only two meals will be required, possibly only one if dried foods are also available on a free-choice basis.

DIETARY DIFFERENCES BETWEEN CATS AND DOGS
You should never feed your cat dog food because dogs and cats have different dietary needs. Cats have a much higher need for fats than dogs, and kittens need more than adult cats. Cats also require unusually high levels of dietary protein as compared with those required by dogs. The foods you choose for your cat must supply these essential components.

ESTABLISHING DAILY INTAKE

Quoting amounts needed is impossible because of the varying factors mentioned. The best way to establish requirements is on an actual consumption basis. Place a small amount of food on the dish and see how quickly this is eaten. If all is devoured within a few minutes, add a little more. Repeat this until the kitten/cat is satiated and walks away from its dish. Do likewise at the other meals and you will quickly establish daily intake.

As the number of meals is decreased, the quantity must be increased at the meals fed.

FOOD AND WATER CONTAINERS

Cornish Rex are not too fussy over what vessels are used for supplying their food and water, but a few tips are useful. Cornish Rex do not like to eat from dirty dishes any more than you would. Their food bowl should be washed after each meal. Water containers should be washed every day and replenished often. Saucers make ideal food plates. Wide feeders from your pet shop are excellent for dried biscuits.

IMPORTANT DON'TS

• Do not let your cat become a fussy eater. Cats are not born fussy but are made that way by their owners. Your cat will not starve if given the correct food, but it may try to convince you otherwise. However, a cat that refuses all foods offered may be ill. Contact your vet.

• Do not give a cat sweet and sticky foods. These provide no benefit and, if eaten, will negatively affect normal appetite for wholesome foods.

• Do not feed vitamin and mineral supplements to either kittens or adults unless under advice from a veterinary surgeon. Excess vitamins and minerals can be as bad for your cat's health as a lack of them. They will create potentially dangerous cellular metabolic imbalances.

• Do not give any questionable foods, such as those that smell or look 'off.' If in doubt, discard them. Always store foods in cool, darkened cupboards. Be sure that all foods from the freezer and refrigerator are fully thawed.

HIGH-QUALITY FOOD

The value of a cat food is determined by its protein/carbohydrate compositions. High-quality foods will contain more protein. The cat is a prime predator and needs a high proportion of protein in its diet.

Pot or polished metal containers are better buys than plastic. They last longer and are easier to keep clean.

The Cornish Rex does not like to place its head into deep food dishes nor do they like their whiskers to touch the inner walls. Ensure dishes are wide and shallow.

MILK AND CATS

Milk, although associated with cats, is not needed once kittenhood has passed. Indeed, too much milk can create skeletal and other problems. Some cats may become quite ill if given too much. They are unable to digest its lactose content. However, small amounts may be appreciated as a treat. Goat's milk, diluted condensed milk and low-lactose milks are better than cow's milk.

DRIED FOOD—MORE WATER
If the cat is only given dried foods, it is essential that its water bowl is always full; it will need to drink more. Be advised that it is best to give both dried and moist food types. This minimises the risk of urological problems created by pH alkalinity associated with dried diets.

WHERE AND WHEN TO FEED
Usually, the best place to feed a cat is in the kitchen. It is important to place food and water dishes as far away from the litter tray as possible. Feeding near the litter tray could deter the cat from eating. Cats also like to eat in quiet comfort. Meals should be spread across the entire day. When the number is reduced to two, these should be given in the morning and evening at convenient times. For the Cornish given outdoor freedom, it is best to feed the main meal in the evening. This encourages the cat to come home at this time. It can then be kept indoors overnight.

Grooming Your
CORNISH REX CAT

From the perspective of grooming, the Cornish Rex has an easy non-matting coat. If brushed every day, it will rarely need combing, though this is beneficial. Brisk brushing followed by a polish, using a chamois leather or piece of silk cloth, will maintain the fur in super condition. If you frequently stroke your Cornish Rex, the natural oils on your hand will give the coat a sleek look.

Regular grooming also enables close examination of the cat for any signs of problems. These include fleas or mites, small wounds, abrasions, swellings and bald areas. The grooming process should include inspection of the cat's ears, teeth and nails.

BRUSHING

Place the cat on a table of an height enabling you to comfortably control and groom the kitty. It can be useful to place white paper on the table. If any fleas are present, you will more easily notice them if they are groomed out of the fur. If the grooming is carried out gently, cats enjoy the experience. You should start when your Cornish Rex is still a kitten. Commence by brushing the fur on the back of the neck. Work along

the back and down the sides, then down the legs and finally the tail. The abdominal area must be brushed more gently, as it is very sensitive.

CLEAN CATS

Cats are self-groomers. They use their barbed tongues and front paws for grooming. Some cats never groom themselves, while others spend up to a third of their waking hours grooming themselves. Licking stimulates certain skin glands that make the coat waterproof.

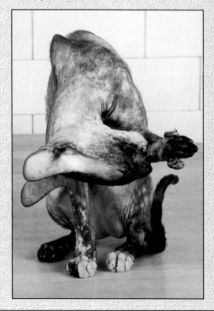

DRY SHAMPOO

A dry bath may be preferred to a wet one during very cold weather or when the cat is not well enough for a water bath. Sprinkle dry shampoo onto the coat and give it a good brushing. This will remove excess grease and dirt without being as thorough as a wet bath. Be very sure that all of the powder is brushed from the fur to avoid potential irritation and consequential scratching.

formulated for cats—do not use one for dogs. This could cause problems on a cat's coat. Baby shampoos are the best alternative. Dry shampoos in powder form are available from pet shops. Alternatives would be talcum powder, powdered chalk or heated bran flakes.

The kitten should be bathed by the time it is six months of age. This will familiarise it with the process before it matures and the

Next, repeat the process using the fine-toothed comb. Then comb against the lie of the hair. This will enable you to see if there are any parasites present. These often favour the tail base or the neck behind the ears. Next, comb with the lie of the fur. Add a final lustre with the chamois.

BATHING

Occasionally, even shorthaired cats may need bathing. This may be of the wet or dry type. For wet baths, using the kitchen sink is preferable to a bath. This saves bending and allows for better control of the cat. To prevent the cat from sliding, use a rubber mat. A spray attachment is more efficient than a jug to wet and rinse the coat. The cat should have its own towels.

The choice of shampoo is important. It ideally should be

GROOMING EQUIPMENT

For total grooming needs, the following are required:

1. Semi-stiff bristle brush or rubber-pinned brush
2. Fine-toothed comb
3. Flea comb
4. Thin chamois leather and/or a silken cloth
5. Pair of guillotine-type nail trimmers
6. Medium-soft toothbrush
7. Cat toothpaste
8. Supply of cotton wool and cotton buds
9. Bottle of baby oil

HAIR-GROWTH FACTORS

Cat's hairs grow denser on the abdomen than on the back. The hairs grow according to both light periodicity (daylight versus dark nights) and temperature. Outdoor cats living in colder climates cast their coats twice a year, in the spring and fall, while most house cats do so all year long.

A coat conditioning spray can be used as a finishing touch following brushing or a bath.

The Cornish Rex's coat does not require extensive grooming, but regular brushing is important.

process degenerates into a pitched battle. Cats have no love of bathing, but can come to accept it if it does not become an unpleasant ordeal.

Grooming should always precede bathing, as this will remove any dead hairs. The key to success lies in ensuring that no water or shampoo is allowed to enter and irritate the eyes or ears.

You should be able to cope single-handed with a kitten. However, it may be prudent to have someone else present just in case the cat proves more of a super cat than a kitten!

The water temperature should be warm, never cold or too hot. Prepare a shampoo and water solution before commencing. Have a large towel at hand. Commence by soaking the fur of the neck, then work along the back, sides, legs and tail. Pour shampoo onto the back and work this in all directions until the cat has been fully shampooed. Next, thoroughly rinse all shampoo away. It is essential that none be left, otherwise it may cause later irritation. Gently but firmly squeeze all water from the coat. The face can be cleaned using a dampened flannel.

Wrap the kitten in the towel and give it a brisk rubbing until it is as dry as possible. It can then be allowed to dry naturally, after which it can be given a final brush and polish. If the cat is normally allowed outdoors, do not allow this for some hours until you are sure the coat is dry. In the colder months, it is best to attend to bathing in the early evening and keep the cat indoors overnight. The use of an hand dryer is not essential on a short-coated breed, but does shorten the drying time.

EARS, EYES AND NAILS

When inspecting the ears, look for any signs of dirt, which can be

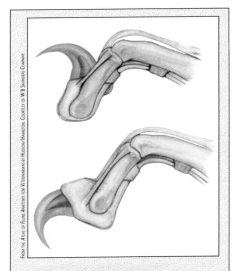

FROM THE ATLAS OF FELINE ANATOMY FOR VETERINARIANS BY HUDSON/HAMILTON, COURTESY OF W B SAUNDERS COMPANY.

RETRACTABLE CLAWS

When at rest, a cat's claws are retracted. The muscles hold the claws in their sheaths. The claw is then extended if the cat wishes to attack prey, defend itself, grab an object or climb. That is why your cat's claws are not always visible. This is true for all species of felines save the cheetah, which is unable to retract its claws, except when it is very young.

HOW DEEP IS YOUR HAIR?

Cat's body hairs grow from the follicles, which are connected to the dermis. Tactile hairs (whiskers) are thicker and longer, originating three times deeper than the normal body hairs.

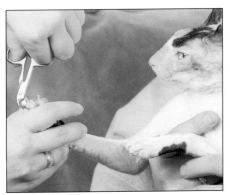

Trimming a cat's nails can be a bit tricky for the uninitiated; you may need a vet or groomer's instruction for the first few tries.

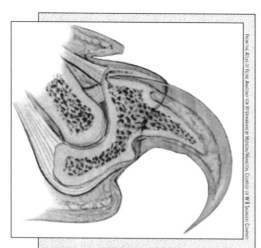

FROM THE ATLAS OF FELINE ANATOMY FOR VETERINARIANS BY HUDSON/HAMILTON. COURTESY OF W.B. SAUNDERS COMPANY.

gently wiped away using a dampened cotton bud or one with just a little baby or vegetable oil on it. Never attempt to probe into the ear. If the ear is very waxed, this may indicate any of various health problems. A visit to the vet is recommended. The corner of the eyes can be wiped gently with damp cotton wool to remove any dust or dirt that occasionally can accumulate.

Inspection of a cat's claws is achieved by firstly restraining it while on its back on your lap or held against your chest. Hold the paw and apply pressure to the

Clean the Cornish Rex's large ears carefully, *never* venturing into the ear canal.

DECLAWING

Declawing is the surgical removal of all of the claw (or nail) and the first toe joint. This practice is heavily frowned upon and even illegal in some countries, such as the United Kingdom. Unfortunately, in some areas of the world, this procedure is still performed. Some owners only have the claws from the front feet removed; others do all four feet.

An alternative surgical procedure is one that removes the tendon that allows the cat to protract its claws. This procedure, referred to as a tendonectomy, as compared to an onychectomy (removal of the claws), is less traumatic for the cat. Claws still must be filed and trimmed after a tendonectomy.

Declawing is not always 100% successful. In two-thirds of the cases, the cats recovered in 72 hours. Only 4–5% of the cats hadn't recovered within a fortnight. About 3% of the cats had their claws grow back!

top of this with your thumb. The nail will appear from its sheath. If the nail needs trimming, use the appropriate trimmers.

It is vital that you do not cut into, or even too close to, the quick, which is a blood vessel. This can be seen as a darker area of the nail in pink-clawed cats. It is more difficult, or not possible, to see the quick in dark-coloured nails. In such instances, trim less. You may need an helper to do the trimming or the holding. If in doubt, let your vet do this for you. If cats have ample access to scratching posts, they will only infrequently, if ever, require their nails to be trimmed.

TEETH

From its youngest days, your kitten should become familiar with having its teeth cleaned. Many owners do not give their cats' teeth the attention they should. This has become progressively more important due to the soft-diet regimens of modern cats. Initially, gently rub the kitten's teeth using a soft cloth on which toothpaste has been placed. This will accustom the kitten to having its teeth touched as well as to the taste of the tooth cleaner. When this is no problem for the kitten, you can progress to a soft toothbrush and ultimately one of medium hardness. Periodically let your vet check the cat's mouth.

GINGIVITIS (Plasmocytic-Lymphocytic Stomatitis)

There are many causes of this condition, but the end result is the same—bad breath, excessive plaque, tooth loss and, almost certainly, pain. The cat salivates excessively, starts to eat less and consequently loses weight. On inspection, the gums are swollen, especially in the areas of the premolar and molar teeth. They bleed easily. There are various treatments, such as antibiotics, immunostimulants and disinfectant mouth gels. However, these invariably prove short-term and merely delay the inevitable treatment of extraction.

Prevention avoids this painful condition. Regular tooth inspection and cleaning, plus provision of hard-food items, such as cat biscuits, achieve this to a large extent. There are also special cat chews made of dried fish that help clean the teeth. They also contain antibacterial enzymes that minimise or prevent secondary bacteria from accumulating. Ask for these at your pet shop or vet's surgery. Gingivitis may commence in kittens, so do not think it is something that only occurs in older cats.

Provide your kitten with a feeling of security in its new home by giving him a cosy bed for a place of its own.

CORNISH REX CAT

One of the outstanding virtues of cats is that they are easy to live with. They are fastidious in their personal habits related to grooming and toilet routines and basically require very little of their owners. Nonetheless, behavioural problems in cats can occur, and an owner needs to understand all of the possible causes and solutions. You may never encounter a single problem with your cat, but it pays to be prepared should your feline charge disrupt your domestic bliss.

THE BASIS OF TRAINING

The most effective means of training a cat is via reinforcement of success. A cat learning from lavish praise of doing what is required will want to repeat the action to gain more affection. There are no potential negative side effects. Conversely, when scolding or another method of discipline is used, there is always the possibility the cat will not relate the punishment to what the owner had intended.

For example, you cannot

SETTING THE GROUND RULES

From the outset, you must determine the ground rules and stick to them. Always remember that your companion's patterns of behaviour begin to form from the moment it first arrives at your home. If the future adult is not to be given outdoor freedom, then do not let it outdoors as a kitten. If any rooms are to be out of bounds to the adult, then do not let the kitten into them. Stability is vital in a cat's life; without it, the result will be stress and its related behavioural changes.

Ground rules of how to handle the kitten and to respect its privacy when sleeping should be instilled into all children. The cat's meals should be given at about the same time each day. This will have the secondary advantage that the pet's toilet habits will be more predictable.

MAN MEETS CAT

Early man, perhaps 8000 years ago, started his symbiotic relationship with domestic cats, *Felis catus* or *Felis domesticus*. The cats killed and ate the rats and mice and probably anything else that crawled and was small, which early man attracted and considered as pests. Early man reciprocated by allowing the cat to sleep in his cave, hut or tent. Cats, being essentially nocturnal, kept the small mammals (rats, mice, etc.) from disturbing the sleep of early man.

As early man evolved to modern man, the domestic cat came along as an aid to pest control. This was especially true of peoples who farmed, as farmers were plagued with rodents. Though most cats were not selectively bred for their predatory skills, it was obvious that those cats that were the best hunters were more successful in evolutionary terms than the cats that were more meek. Modern cats have changed very little from the cats from which they descended. There are still, today, cats that are very predatory, attacking small mammals and birds; there are also meek cats which, unless fed by their owners, would perish in a competitive cat society.

It has been shown repeatedly that if kittens are socialised in a proper manner, they will become peaceful pets. If the kittens are not socialised properly, they revert immediately to their aggressive, predatory behaviours.

CATS AND OTHER PETS

If you already have a pet cat or dog, or almost any other animal that isn't small, creeping or crawling, your cat usually can be socialised so that the other pet and the cat will tolerate each other. In many cases, cats and dogs become quite friendly and attached to each other, often making frequent physical contacts, sleeping together or even sharing each other's toy.

discipline for something done in the past. The past is anything much longer than a few minutes ago. If you call the cat to you and punish it for something done hours earlier, it cannot relate to that action. It will relate the discipline to the act of going to you when called! This will create insecurity in the pet, increasing the risk that more problems will develop.

REMEDIAL METHODS

When faced with a problem, firstly try to pinpoint the likely cause(s). Next, consider the remedial options. Be sure that these remedies will not result in negative side effects linked to you. Always be the paragon of patience. Some problems may be extremely complex and deeply rooted within the cat's behaviour patterns. As such, they are habits not easily changed and often difficult to analyse. In discussing

A properly behaved Cornish Rex is a beautiful addition to the family. This is a lovely lilac.

FERAL CATS

Feral cats, as a general rule, are undernourished. They spend most of their time searching for food. Consequently, those feral cats that have kittens spend less time with their kittens than do well-nourished cats. It has been shown that kittens born to feral mothers are usually unsocial and show little affection for their mothers. Obviously, they would show a similar lack of affection for a human. That's one of the reasons that feral kittens make poor pets and should neither be adopted nor taken into your home. Kittens that for any reason are separated from their mothers at the age of two weeks develop an attitude of fear and wariness. They escape from contact with other cats and humans and can even be dangerous if they feel trapped.

Your Cornish Rex is constantly alert and on the move, so you must be equally aware of what your cat is getting into.

become apparent from the time the kitten gets to its new home, or it may develop at any time during its life. So, let us start from the beginning and try to avoid the situation.

Until you are satisfied that the kitten is using its litter tray, do not give it access to carpeted rooms. The youngster should already have been litter-trained well before you obtained it. You should buy a litter tray similar to the one with which it is already familiar. It is also important that the same type of litter is used, at

the following problems, it is hoped that you will understand the basic ways to correct other unwanted patterns of behaviour that might occur. But always remember, it is far better to avoid a problem than to correct it.

THE LITTER TRAY

A very common problem for some owners is that their cat starts to attend to its toiletry needs anywhere other than in its litter tray. The problem may least initially. Place the tray in a quiet spot so the kitten has privacy when attending to its needs.

A kitten will need to relieve itself shortly after it has eaten, exercised or been sleeping. Watch it carefully at these times. If it stoops to attend to its needs other than in the litter tray, calmly lift it into its tray and scratch at the litter. Never shout or panic the kitty by making a sudden rush for it. If it does what is hoped, give it lots of praise. If it steps out of the tray, gently

TIDY TOILETING

During the kitten's stay in the nest box, the mother will assist or even stimulate bowel and urine elimination, at least for the first month of the kitten's life. The mother also does the clean-up work in the nest box. But once the kitten is older, it becomes capable of relieving itself out of the nest box. Usually the kitten likes sand, soft earth or something that seems absorbent and is easily moved with its paws. By the time the kitten is two months old, it should develop the discipline of covering its elimination. Not all kittens develop this discipline, though the use of an absorbent clay litter seems to be helpful in developing this discipline in young cats. Your local pet shop will have various cat litters for sale.

CAUSES OF LITTER-BOX PROBLEMS

1. The litter tray is dirty. Cats never like to use a previously fouled tray.
2. The litter has been changed to one of a different texture that the cat does not like. Generally the finer-grained litters are the most favoured.
3. A scented litter is being used to mask odours. The cat may not like the scent. Such litters should not be necessary if the tray is regularly cleaned.
4. The tray is regularly cleaned, but an ammonium or pine-based disinfectant is being used. This may aggravate the cat's sensitive nasal mucous membranes. Additionally, the phenols in pine are dangerous to cats. If bleach is used, be certain that it is thoroughly rinsed.
5. The litter tray is located too close to the cat's food and water bowls. Cats do not like to eat near litter trays or to defecate/urinate close to their feeding areas.
6. Another cat or free-roaming pet has been added to the household and is causing the cat stress. In multi-cat households, two or more trays may be needed.
7. There is insufficient litter in the tray. There should be about 5 cms (2 ins) of litter depth.
8. The cat has developed a fear of using the tray due to an upsetting experience. For instance, the owner may have caught the cat as it finished using the tray in order that it could be given a medicine. Children may be disturbing it while it is relieving itself.
9. The cat is ill (or elderly) and is unable to control its bowel movements. Veterinary attention is required.
10. The cat, because of one or more of the previous problems, has established other more favourable areas.

place it back in for a few seconds.

If nothing happens, be patient and wait, and then repeat the process. If it fouls the kitchen floor when you are not watching, simply clean this up and wait for the next opportunity to transport the kitten to its tray. It rarely takes long for a kitten to consistently use the litter tray. Be very sure that the tray is kept spotless. Cats have no more desire to use a fouled toilet than you do. Every few days, give the cat tray a good wash using soapy water and always rinse it thoroughly. Allow it to dry, then fill the tray with litter to a depth of about 4–5 cms (1.5–2 inches).

By identifying the cause(s) of litter-box problems, the correction is often self-evident. However, once the cause has been corrected, this is only part of the solution. Next, the habit of fouling other places must be overcome. Where possible, do not let the cat enter rooms that it has started to foul until the odour has had time to disperse fully. Wash the area of the fouling, then treat carpets and soft furnishings with an odour neutraliser (not an air freshener) from your pet shop or vet.

If the cat cannot be prevented from entering certain rooms, then cover previously fouled areas with plastic sheeting or tinfoil, or rinse the fouled area with white vinegar (which cats hate!). Also, place a litter tray in the fouled room while the retraining is underway. It may help if a different size, type or colour of tray is used.

SCENT MARKING

Both sexes scent mark, though males are more prolific. It is a means of advertising their presence in a territory, thus an integral part of their natural behaviour. Spraying is usually done against a vertical surface. It tells other males that the individual is residing in that territory. Alternatively, it will tell a female that a male lives close by—or it will tell the male that a female is in the area. It is thus a very important part of a cat's social language.

Neutered cats have little need to mark their territory or leave their 'calling card' to attract mates. They are far less likely to spray than those not altered. However, scent marking may commence when the cat is attempting to assert its position in the household.

To overcome the problem of scent marking, you first need to try to identify if there is an obvious specific cause. In multi-cat households, it also requires positive identification of the sprayer(s) and the favoured spraying surface. Giving the cat

CAUSES OF SCENT MARKING

1. Another cat or pet has been introduced to the household. It may be bullying the resident cat. This problem may resolve itself when the two get to know each other. The more cats there are, the longer it may take for the situation to be resolved. Much will depend on the space within which the cats may roam and whether they are able to avoid those they dislike.
2. The birth of a new family member may annoy the cat for a while, especially if its owner suddenly gives it less attention.
3. A friend staying in the home for a few days may not like cats. If 'shooed' away a number of times, the cat may feel it should assert its position and mark it.

4. If the cat is given outdoor freedom, a bully may have moved into the territory. Having lost control of its own garden, the pet may assert its territorial boundaries within its home. If a cat flap is used, another cat may be entering the home and this will trigger the resident to scent mark.

Keep your cat's claws out of the furniture by providing him with something appropriate on which to scratch.

more freedom may help, and its own sleeping place if it does not have one. Covering the sprayed surface with plastic sheeting or a cloth impregnated with a scent the cat does not like (such as lemon, pepper or bleach), may be successful. Spraying the cat with a water pistol when catching it in the action is a common ploy. Veterinary treatment with the hormone progesterone may prove effective—discuss this with your vet.

SCRATCHING
Scratching is a normal feline characteristic. Unfortunately, house cats tend to destroy the furniture to satisfy their need to scratch. Feral or outdoor cats usually attack a tree because trees are readily accessible and the bark of the tree suits their needs perfectly. If the outdoor cat lives in a pride, it will scratch more than a solitary feral cat. The reasons for this are known. When

cats scratch, they leave telltale marks. Parts of the nails' sheaths exudate from glands located between their claws, and the visual aspects are the marks that cats leave to impress or advertise their presence.

Cat owners should not consider the scratching as an aggressive behavioural disorder. It is normal for cats to scratch. Keeping your cat's claws clipped or filed so they are as short as possible without causing bleeding may inhibit scratching. Your vet can teach you how to do this. Clipping and filing should be started when the kitten is very young. Starting this when the cat has matured is much more difficult and may even be dangerous.

THE TRUTH ABOUT CATS AND DOGS
Cats are unique in having the scrotum fully haired, a marked difference from their canine counterparts. This led one early observer to say that cats were not small dogs! Dogs were domesticated well before cats since cats only served to protect the abode of the owner from rodents, while dogs served as guards, hunters, herders, exterminators and loyal companions that were readily trainable. Cats have always been more independent and less trainable.

There are ways to control annoying cat scratching. Certainly, the easiest way is to present your cat with an acceptable scratching post. These are usually available at most pet shops. The post should be covered with a material that is to your cat's liking. If your cat has already indicated what it likes to scratch, it usually is a good idea to cover the post with this same material. Veterinary surgeons often suggest that you use sandpaper, as this will reduce the cat's nails quickly and it will not have the urge to scratch. Certainly using hemp, carpeting, cotton towelling or bark is worth a try. Once the cat uses the post, it usually will have neither a desire nor a need to scratch any place else.

Besides the physical need to scratch, cats have a psychological need to scratch. This is evidenced by where they scratch versus what they scratch. Often cats prefer semi-darkness. Some prefer flat surfaces and not vertical surfaces. Some prefer public areas in which their human friends are present instead of secluded areas. It may be stress-related, as with scent marking, because scratching is another territory-marking behaviour. In any case, the idea is to get your cat to scratch the post and not the carpets, furniture, drapes or duvet on your bed.

Introduce your cat to the post by rubbing its paws on the post, hoping it will take the hint. Oftentimes the cat voluntarily attacks the post. Unfortunately, oftentimes it doesn't. If you catch your cat scratching in a forbidden area, startle it with a loud shout, banging a folded newspaper against your hand or something else that will take its attention away from scratching. Never hit the cat. This will only get a revengeful reaction that might be dangerous.

Scratching is to cats what chewing is to dogs...a physical need and an enjoyable activity.

RUBBISH RUMMAGING

Cats are inquisitive and may decide to have a good look through any interesting rubbish bins that are exuding enticing odours. Normally, the answer is to remove the bin. However, if the attraction always seems to be to the kitchen rubbish, there may be a nutritional problem. The cat may be searching for food because it is not getting enough food or is being underfed! The cat may alternatively be receiving an unbalanced diet and is trying to satisfy its inner need for a given missing ingredient.

Another possibility, and one which may be more appropriate to the indoors-only cat, is boredom or loneliness. These conditions can only be remedied by greater interaction between owner and cat and/or obtaining a companion feline.

Clearly, the cause should be identified. The immediate solution is to place the rubbish in a cupboard or similar place that is out of the cat's reach. This type of solution is called removal of the re-enforcer. It is a common method of overcoming problems across a number of unwanted behaviours. However, it does not correct the underlying problem, which must still be addressed.

The first-time cat owner should not think that all of the problems discussed will likely be encountered. They are only met when the cat's environment is lacking in some way. Always remember that the older cat may have problems with bowel control. An extra litter tray at another location in the home will usually remedy this situation. Finally, if a problem is found and you are not able to remedy it yourself, do seek the advice of your vet or breeder.

The Cornish Rex is very aware of its surroundings and ready to spring to action whenever something sparks its interest... which is quite often!

CORNISH REX CAT

While the idea of becoming a breeder may appeal to many owners, the reality is more difficult than is often appreciated. It requires dedication, considerable investment of time and money and the ability to cope with many heart-wrenching decisions and failures.

It would be quite impossible to discuss the complexities of practical breeding in only one short chapter, so we will consider the important requirements of being a breeder plus basic feline reproductive information. This will enable you to better determine if, indeed, this aspect of the hobby is for you.

BEING A BREEDER

Apart from great affection for the breed, a successful breeding programme requires quantifiable objectives. Foremost among these is the rearing of healthy kittens free from known diseases. Next is the desire to produce offspring that are as good as, indeed better than, their parents.

Such objectives ensure that a breeder will endeavour to maintain standards and reduce or remove from the breed population any instances of dangerous diseases and conditions. Only

TOO MANY CATS

There are already too many cats in the world. In many countries, thousands of pathetic-looking felines can be seen wandering the streets in a badly emaciated state. They lead tormented lives and have become a major social problem in many areas. There can be no excuse for these feral populations in developed Western nations. Quite frankly, some people who own cats, including some pedigreed owners, lack a sense of responsibility.

Cats allowed to roam in a non-neutered state are by far the main reason for the overpopulation problem. Unless a cat is of show or breeding quality, there is not a single justification for it to be bred or to remain in a non-neutered state. If your cat was purchased as a pet, you should help to resolve this global problem by having it neutered at the earliest possible date. This will make it a far healthier, happier and less problematic pet.

The goal of breeding is to produce offspring that exhibit the same, or better, quality as their parents by planning matings that will pass on the parent's best traits.

demanding, especially once they are over three weeks of age. Rearing, vaccination, registration and veterinary bills will be costly. Any thoughts of profit should be dispelled. Homes must be found for the kittens, which will entail

stock registered and tested free of major diseases should ever be used. Adopting such a policy helps to counteract those who breed from inferior and often unhealthy cats.

To be a successful breeder, you will need to become involved in the show competition side of the hobby. Only via this route will you be able to determine if your programme is successful or not. Always remember that even the top-winning breeders still produce quite an high percentage of kittens that will only be of pet quality. There will be many disappointments along the road to even modest success.

THE DISADVANTAGES OF BREEDING

There are many rewards to be gained from breeding, but the disadvantages should also be carefully considered. Kittens are

TOM FOOLERY

A non-neutered male cat kept as a single pet has little or no value for breeding purposes. It must be exhibited so it can gain some fame. The owner must have modern facilities to house both males and females. Females are always serviced at the home of the stud owner. This is extra responsibility and cost.

Such a male cannot be given any freedom to roam. If the tom is kept indoors, its scent-marking odours will often become intolerable. Even kept outdoors in a suitable cat pen, it will spray regularly to attract the attention of any females in the area. Toms are more assertive and often more aggressive than neutered males. If they are allowed any outdoor freedom, they will become involved in battles with the local toms. Consequently, they will soon lose their handsome looks!

Most cat breeders do not even keep males because of the problems and costs they entail. These cats are best kept in catteries where the owners have the time, the funds and everything else needed to justify their retention.

CAT CALLS

Females left in a non-spayed state are far more at risk from diseases and infections of the uterus. When in heat, the female becomes unusually affectionate and provocative. Her calls, a sound once heard never forgotten, can become extremely annoying if she is left unmated.

receiving many telephone calls—some at very inconvenient hours.

Many potential buyers will prove to be either unsuitable or 'time wasters' looking for the cheapest pedigreed cat obtainable. Kittens may die, while cats of any age could test positive for a major disease. They may have to be put to sleep or given to a caring person who understands the problem.

Owning a number of cats will mean investing in cat pens. When females come into heat, they will try to escape and mate with any local tom with a twinkle in his eye! Their scent and calls will attract roving Romeos, who will gather near your home and involve themselves in a series of raucous battles. Holidays and matings will need to be planned around hoped-for litter dates. All in all, owning only one or two breeding females is a major commitment.

Before deciding whether breeding really is something you

want to do, what would make good sense would be to neuter the pet and then become an exhibitor. When you have exhibited a number of times, your knowledge of cats will be greater, as will your contacts. You will be more aware of what quality is all about and what it will cost for a well-bred female. It will be like an apprenticeship. Whether you then become a breeder, remain an

CAVEAT EMPTOR

When purchasing a kitten for breeding, make certain that the seller knows what your intentions are. If a kitten is registered on the non-active register, this means that it was not considered by its breeder to be good enough for breeding. Any kittens bred from such a cat cannot be registered. You should also check that the mother of the kitten/young adult in which you are interested has tested negative for FeLV, FIP and FIV and that all vaccinations are current.

exhibitor or prefer life as a pet owner, you will be glad you heeded the words of advice given here.

STOCK SELECTION

Stock selection revolves around health, quality, sex and age. Before these are discussed, it should be stated that many beginners unwisely rush this process. It is essential that ample time be devoted to researching from whom to purchase breeding stock. This decision will influence a novice breeder's entire future endeavours.

HEALTH

Cats should only be obtained from a breeder whose stock has been tested negative for the cat diseases known as FeLV, FIP and FIV. The stock should be current on all vaccinations and worm treatments. Additionally, its blood type should be known so as to avoid incompatibility problems.

QUALITY

This must come in two forms. One is in the individual cat's appearance; the other is in its genetic ability to pass on the quality of its parents. The best way of obtaining these paired needs is to obtain initial stock from a breeder having a proven record of success with the Cornish Rex. Being well-acquainted with the breed's standard will be

> **THE BREEDING QUEEN**
>
> A female used for breeding purposes is called a queen. The principal requirement of such a cat is that she is an excellent example of the breed. This does not mean that she must be a show winner. Many a winning exhibition cat has proved to have little breeding value. This is because a show cat gains success purely on its appearance; however, it may not pass those looks to its offspring.
>
> A good breeding female may lack that extra something needed to be a top winner. Yet, she may pass on most of her excellent features to her offspring. Much will depend on the breeding line from which she was produced. Therefore, any potential breeder must research existing breeders to ascertain which have good track records of producing consistently high-quality cats. In truth, and sadly, few newcomers in their haste to become breeders make this extra effort. This can result in becoming disillusioned if the female produces only average to inferior kittens.

advantageous when seeking foundation stock. A female show cat attains her titles based on her appearance, but she may not pass on those looks to her offspring. Another cat that is very sound may pass on most of her good points and thus be more valuable for breeding. Of course, all litters will be influenced by the quality of the tom used. He will account for 50% of the offspring's genes. When viewing a litter of kittens, never forget that it is the result of the genes of two cats.

THE MALE STUD

The selection of a suitable stud should have been planned months before, as it can take some time to find the best male to use. It is preferred that the breeding lines of the stud are compatible with those of the female, meaning that both pedigrees will carry a number of the same individuals in them. This is termed line-breeding. The ideal male will excel in those features that are considered weak in the female. You may read in other books that if a female is weak in a given feature, the ideal stud will be the total opposite. However, this can be misleading.

If the female has an overly long tail, what you do not need is a stud with a short tail. Rather, his tail should be as near the ideal length as possible. Genetically, this will improve tail length in your line without introducing unwanted genetic variance in your stock. Compensatory matings, such as short tail to long tail, will create such a variance. Once a male has been selected, ensure that all his papers and vaccinations are in order. The female will be taken to the stud and left with him for a few days.

SEX

The beginner should obtain only females. The best advice is to commence with just one very sound female. By the time you have exhibited her and gained more knowledge about the finer points of the breed, you will be better able to judge what true quality is all about. By then, you also will have made many contacts on the show circuit. Alternatively, you may decide that breeding is not for you and will have invested the minimum of time and money.

A male is not needed until a breeder has become established. Even then, owning one is not essential to success. There is no

Quality breeding starts with quality stock. This is a typical red tabby.

NEWBORN KITTENS

Most kittens are born with body hair. Their ears and eyes, however, remain closed for about two weeks, though some ears and eyes become functional after 72 hours. Kittens should be allowed to nurse for seven weeks, longer if they will not readily eat and drink from a plate. If allowed to nurse, most kittens will stay on their mother's milk for two months or more.

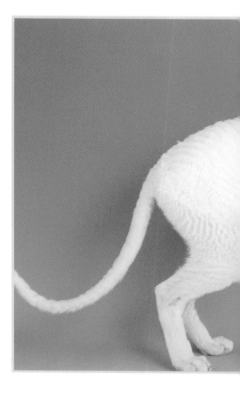

shortage of quality studs. Males create many problems that the novice can do without. Once experience is gained is the time to decide if owning a male would be of any particular benefit.

AGE

There is no specific age at which stock should be purchased, but the following are suggested:

1. Most people purchase young kittens so they can enjoy them. However, with such youngsters, their ultimate quality is harder to assess.
2. Chances are improved if a kitten has already won awards in shows. This will be when she is 14 weeks to 9 months of age, but she will be more costly.
3. A quality young female that has already produced offspring is a prudent choice but will be the most expensive option.

THE BREEDING PROCESS

Sexual maturity in cats may come as early as four months of age. Breeding should not be considered until the female is at least 12 months old, especially in the slow-maturing breeds such as those of Persian and European stock ancestry. A young cat barely out of her kitten stage may not have the required physical or psychological stability to produce and raise a vigorous litter. After her first heat, a female will normally come into heat again every two to three weeks and

ing. At this time, they also will be sampling solid foods. By eight weeks, they can be vaccinated and neutered if required. Weaning normally commences by the age of six weeks and is completed within two to three weeks.

Kittens can go to a new home when 12 weeks old, though 14 to 16 weeks is preferred. During this period, you must decide if you wish to register the kittens or merely 'declare' them. This allows them to be registered at a later time. Obtain the necessary information and forms from your cat-registration authority. You should also consider the benefits of registering your own breeder prefix. This, however, is only worthwhile if you intend to breed on a more than casual basis. If you have decided that certain kittens are unsuitable for showing/breeding, do consider early neutering.

A blue-eyed white, displaying a marvellous rex coat.

continue to do so until mated. The actual oestrous period lasts three to eight days. It is during this time that she is receptive to a male.

Once the mating has been successful, the time between fertilisation and birth of the young, known as the gestation period, is in the range of 59 to 67 days, 63 or 64 days being typical. The litter size generally will be two to five. Kittens are born blind and helpless, but develop rapidly. Their eyes open about the seventh day. By 21 days, they start explor-

THE HEAT IS ON

Most female cats reach sexual maturity by the time they are 28 weeks old. Females normally accept males from late winter to early fall, about a six-month period. They have a reproductive cycle of about two weeks and are in heat for about one of the two weeks. Intercourse causes the female to ovulate and pregnancy may last for about 64 days, perhaps longer in cold climates and shorter in the tropics.

Whether as an exhibitor or spectator, you can experience the full realm of the fancy at a cat show. This is an example of a brown mackerel tabby.

Exhibiting Your
CORNISH REX CAT

Without shows, the cat fancy could not exist. There would be only an handful of breeds as compared with today's ever-growing list. There would be fewer colour patterns and far less cat awareness. Given the great importance of shows to the cat fancy, it is perhaps a little surprising, and disappointing, that the majority of cat owners have never visited a feline exhibition.

Shows such as the National and the Supreme of Britain, or their equivalents in other countries, are the shop windows of the world of domestic cats. They are meeting places where breeders from all over the country compete to establish how well their breeding programmes are developing. A show is also a major social event on the cat calendar.

Whether a potential pet owner or breeder of the future, you should visit one or two shows. It is a great day out for the whole family. Apart from the wonderful selection of breeds and colours, there are also many trade stands. If a product is available, it will be seen at the large exhibitions.

Many of the national clubs

EXAMPLES OF CLASSES AT SHOWS

Open	Cats of the specified breed.
Novice	Cats that have never won a first prize.
Limit	Cats that have not won more than first prizes.
Junior	Cats over nine months of age but less than two years on the day of the show.
Senior	Cats over two years old.
Visitors	Cats living a given distance away from the show venue.
Assessment	Experimental breeds, which have approved standards.
Aristocrat	Cats with one or two Challenge Certificates, so are not yet full Champions (or Premiers for neuters).

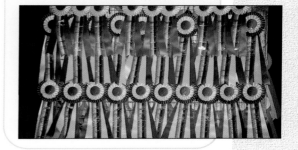

A beautiful exhibit in chocolate smoke.

and magazines have stands. The two major shows mentioned are held in the winter months, usually November and December. However, there are hundreds of other shows staged during the year in various parts of the country. They range from small local club events to major championship breed shows and are usually advertised in the cat magazines. Your ruling cat association can also supply a list of shows.

SHOW ORGANISATION

So you will have some idea of how things are organised, the following information will be helpful. You will learn even more by purchasing the show catalogue. This contains the names and addresses of the exhibitors and details of their cats. It also lists the prizes, indicates the show

'VETTING IN'

In England, cats are examined by a veterinary surgeon upon arrival at a show to make sure that they appear healthy. This process is called 'vetting in.' If the cat is rejected, it cannot be exhibited again until it receives a 'clearance certificate.' The possible reasons for rejection are stated in the rule book, which can be obtained at the show.

regulations and carries many interesting advertisements.

A major show revolves around three broad categories of cats:
1. Unaltered cats, meaning those that are capable of breeding.
2. Neuters.
3. Non-pedigreed cats.

There is, thus, the opportunity for every type of cat, from the best Cornish Rex to the everyday 'moggie' pets, to take part. These three broad categories are divided into various sections. For example, the unaltered and neuters are divided into their respective sections, such as Longhair, Semi-Longhair, British, Foreign, Siamese and so on.

There are many more classes other than those mentioned. These include club classes and those for kittens and non-pedigreed cats as well as 'fun' classes that will bring amusement to all cat lovers and spark the imagination of the most creative fanciers.

JUDGING

There are two ways cats can be judged. One is pen judging, the other is bench or ring judging. In Britain, pen judging is the normal method, though bench judging is used for Best in Show. In pen judging, the judge moves around the cat pens. The cat gaining the most points when compared to the standard wins. In bench judging, stewards take the cats to the judge.

A show cat must be accustomed to handling, as judging is an hands-on procedure.

This blue tortie displays a coat in top condition, a necessity for a show exhibit.

ON THE CONTINENT AND BEYOND...

In Britain, the title of UK Grand Champion or Premier is won in competition with other Grand titleholders. In mainland Europe, cats can become International Champions. More British cats are expected to become International Champions with the recent introduction of passports for cats, allowing cats to compete more freely on the Continent and beyond. In countries other than Britain, the way in which shows are organised and titles achieved do differ somewhat. However, they broadly follow the outline discussed here.

If a cat wins its class, it then competes against other class winners. By this process of elimination, a cat may go on to win the Best of Breed award. It then competes against other breed winners for the Best in Group award. The group winners compete for the Best in Show award.

A breeder can gather a number of awards during the course of a show. Even those who do not own the very best cats can take pride in gaining second, third, fourth and recommended, especially if won at the larger shows. By progression, the top cat at a show will win its class, its breed and its section, and

Visiting a show enables spectators to see the range of colours in which the breed is seen. This is a red tabby Cornish Rex.

ultimately become the Best in Show exhibit. The titles a cat can win commence with that of Champion (or Premier in the case of neuters). A Grand Champion is made after winning in competition with others of its same status. The same applies to a Grand Premier. The judging system may vary from one country to another but the basis remains as outlined.

THE SHOW CAT

When a cat is seen preening in its pen, the hard work that has gone into its preparation is rarely appreciated. Exhibits must be in peak condition and their coats in full bloom. The potential exhibit must be trained gradually to spend hours within its show pen. It must display no fear or aggression towards strangers, such as the stewards or the judges. These must be able to physically examine the cat, including its ears and teeth; it also involves being lifted into the air. If a cat scratches or bites a judge, or any other show official, it is automatically withdrawn from the show. A repeat of this in the future would result, in most instances, in the cat's show career being terminated by the ruling association.

Apart from being comfortable with people peering into its pen, the cat must be able to endure long journeys to the show venue. Unless trained, the cat may become a nervous, aggressive

BECOMING AN EXHIBITOR

Before any hobbyist enters a show, he is advised to join a local cat club. Here, hobbyists will meet local breeders who will not only assess their cats for them but also provide help on many other topics. The novice exhibitor could attend one or two shows with an exhibitor in order to learn the ropes. During this period, he can become familiar with the show rules and regulations. These are quite extensive, intended to safeguard the best interests of the hobby, the exhibitors and, most importantly, the cats.

It is of interest to note that some breeders own cats in partnership with other fanciers. This is useful when one person enjoys the breeding side and the other the exhibition side. It enables both to be really involved in the hobby to a level that might not have been possible for either on his own. So, whether you fancy being an exhibitor or you just love cats, do make a point of visiting the next major show in your area.

feline that will have a very short show career.

Obviously, the cat must display quality. This means having none of the major faults that would prevent it from gaining a first prize. These are listed in the breed standard. The meaning of quality is very subjective. You

A brown Cornish Rex with colour-points similar to those of a Siamese cat.

do not need to own a potential champion to be a successful exhibitor. The cat also must be registered with the association under whose rules the show is being run. In Britain, this will be the Governing Council of the Cat Fancy (GCCF) or The Cat Association of Britain.

As in anything competitive, exhibits can gain prizes at the lower levels of an hobby without having any realistic chance of top awards in the major shows. Owning such exhibits is often part of a top breeder/exhibitor's portfolio from his early days in the hobby. Others may never

The tortie and white coloration.

CLASSES FOR NON-PEDIGREED CATS

For non-pedigreed cats there are many classes, which include those for single colours, bicolours, tabbies, half-pedigreed, and so on. In this section, are many delightful classes, such as those for cats owned by pensioners, by young children (by age group), best original stray or rescued cat, best personality, most unusual looking, most photogenic and best older cat. Within this cat section can be seen some truly gorgeous felines. There is no doubt that the pet classes have been the springboard that has launched many a top breeder into the world of pedigreed cats.

move beyond the smaller shows but still gain reputations for owning sound stock. They thoroughly enjoy being involved at their given level.

If the idea of exhibiting appeals to you, the best way to make a start is to join a local club. There you not only will be advised on all procedures but also will be able to make many new friends. Exhibiting can be costly in cash and time, but you can focus on the more local shows while attending the larger ones as a visitor.

An elegant black
and white Cornish
Rex.

An occasional itch is normal, but constant scratching may indicate a skin problem. If you notice your Cornish Rex's scratching more than usual, a visit to the vet is advised.

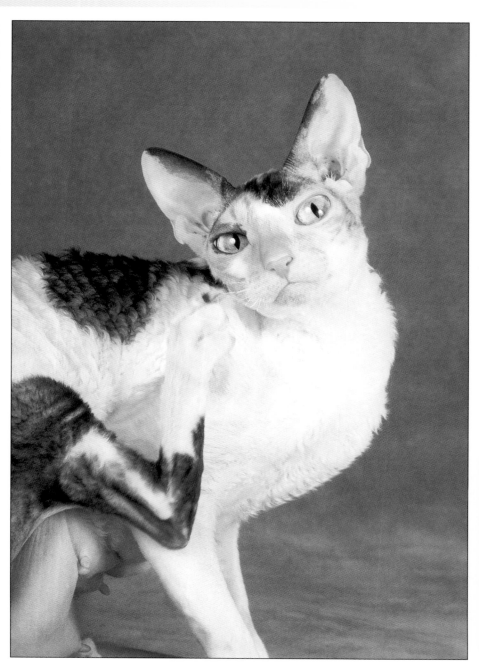

CORNISH REX CAT

Maintaining a cat in the peak of good health revolves around the implementation of a sound husbandry strategy. At the basic level, this means being responsible about feeding, cleanliness, and grooming. However, in spite of an owner's best efforts in these matters, cats may still become ill due to other causes. Although owners can attempt to prevent, identify and react to problems, only a vet is qualified to diagnose and suggest and/or effect remedies. Attempts by owners or 'informed' friends to diagnose and treat for specific diseases are dangerous and potentially life-threatening to the cat.

SELECTING A VETERINARY SURGEON

Your selection of a veterinary surgeon should be based upon his

With an healthy start and a routine of regular health care, this Cornish kitten has a long life to look forward to!

skills with small animals, his knowledge of cats (and Rexes in particular) and his personality, as well as his convenience to your home. You want a vet who is close because you might have emergencies or need to make multiple visits for treatments. You want a vet who has services that you might require such as nail clipping and bathing, as well as sophisticated pet supplies and a good reputation for ability and responsiveness. There is nothing more frustrating than having to wait a day or more to get a response from your veterinary surgeon.

A LONG, HEALTHY LIFE
As veterinary surgeons make medical advances in the health care of cats, the longevity of the typical house cat is improving. Certainly ages between 15 and 18 years are not uncommon, and reports of cats living more than 20 years are predictable.

KEEPING YOUR CAT HEALTHY
Although there are a multitude of ailments, diseases and accidents that could befall a cat, all but the most minor of problems can be avoided with good management. The following tips are a recipe for keeping your cat in the peak of health.

- Make sure it is vaccinated and in other ways protected from each of the major diseases. It must also receive annual boosters to maintain immunity.
- Have periodic checks made by your vet to see if your cat has worms.
- Ensure that the cat receives an adequate diet that is both appealing and balanced.
- Have the kitten neutered if it is not to be used for breeding.
- Ensure that the cat's litter tray, food/water vessels and grooming tools are always maintained in spotless condition.
- Do not let your cat out overnight or when you are away from the home.
- Always wash your hands after gardening or petting other people's pets.
- Groom your cat daily. If this is done, you will more readily notice fleas or other problems than if grooming were done less frequently.
- Never try to diagnose and treat problems that are clearly of an internal type. Remember, even the most informed of breeders is not a vet and unable to reliably diagnose problems for you or advise treatments. Contact your vet.
- If you are ever in doubt about the health of your cat, do not delay in discussing your concerns with your vet. Delays merely allow problems to become more established.

All veterinary surgeons are licenced and their diplomas and/or certificates should be displayed in their waiting rooms. There are, however, many veterinary specialities that usually require further studies and internships. There are specialists in heart problems (veterinary cardiologists), skin problems (veterinary dermatologists), teeth and gum problems (veterinary dentists), eye problems (veterinary ophthalmologists) and x-rays (veterinary radiologists), as well as vets who have specialities in reproduction, nutrition and behaviour. Most veterinary surgeons do routine surgery, such as neutering and stitching up wounds.

When the problem affecting your cat is serious, it is not unusual or impudent to get another medical opinion, although in Britain you are obliged to advise the vets concerned about this. You might also want to compare costs among several veterinary surgeons. Sophisticated health care and veterinary services can be very costly. It is not infrequent that important decisions are based upon financial considerations.

BLOOD GROUP INCOMPATIBILITY (BGI)

In recent years, blood group incompatibility has become the focus of scientists, vets and breeders. Its importance to pet owners is when transfusions are needed. For breeders, it probably accounts for a large percentage of kittens that die from fading kitten syndrome. Scientifically, the problem is called neonatal erythrolysis, meaning the destruction of red blood cells in newly born offspring.

Cats have two blood groups, A & B. Group A is dominant to B (which is genetically called recessive). When the antibodies of group-B mothers are passed to group-A kittens, via her colostrum milk, they destroy red blood cells. Death normally follows within a few days.

Most domestic cats tested are group A. However, national and regional differences display a variation in which 1-6% may be of type B. In pedigree breeds, it has been found that the number of group B cats varies significantly. The following breeds, based on present available data, have the indicated percentage incidence of group B blood type.

0%	Siamese, Burmese and Oriental Shorthair
1-5%	Maine Coon, Manx and Norwegian Forest
10-20%	Abyssinian, Birman, Japanese Bobtail, Persian, Scottish Fold and Somali
25-50%	Cornish Rex, Devon Rex, British Shorthair, Exotic Shorthair

The clear implication to breeders is to establish their cats' blood group, via testing, and conduct appropriate matings. These should not result in group-B mothers nursing group-A kittens. The safe matings are:

1. Group-A males   x   A females
2. Group-B males   x   A or B females
3. Group-A females   x   A or B males
4. Group-B females   x   B males

Breeders are advised to seek further information before embarking on stock purchase and breeding programmes.

THE RIB CAGE
Cats usually have 13 pairs of ribs. The ribs in the middle are longer than the ribs on either end (or beginning) of the rib cage. The first nine ribs are joined to the chest bone (sternum) with costal cartilages. Ribs 10, 11 and 12 are also associated with cartilage, which contributes to the costal arch. The thirteenth rib is called the floating rib and its cartilage is separate from the other ribs.

PREVENTATIVE MEDICINE
It is much easier, less costly and more effective to practise preventative medicine than to fight bouts of illness and disease. Properly bred kittens come from parents who were selected based upon their genetic disease profile. Their mothers should have been vaccinated, free of all internal and external parasites and properly nourished. For these reasons, a visit to the veterinary surgeon who cared for the queen is recommended. The queen can pass on disease resistance to her kittens, which can last for eight to ten weeks. She can also pass on parasites and many infections. That's why it is helpful to know about the queen's health.

VACCINATIONS
Most vaccinations are given by injection and should only be

HEALTH AND VACCINATION TIMETABLE

Age	6 wks	8 wks	10 wks	12 wks	16 wks	6 mos	1 yr
Worm control	✔	✔	✔		✔		
Neutering						✔	
Rhinotracheitis	✔	✔		✔	✔		✔
Panleukopenia	✔	✔		✔			✔
Calcivirus		✔			✔		✔
Feline Leukaemia				✔			✔
Feline Infectious Peritonitis				✔	✔		✔
Faecal evaluation						✔	
Feline Immunodeficiency testing							✔
Feline Leukaemia testing				✔			✔
Dental evaluation		✔				✔	
Rabies				✔	✔		✔

Vaccinations are not instantly effective. It takes about two weeks for the cat's immune system to develop antibodies. Most vaccinations require annual booster shots. Your veterinary surgeon should guide you in this regard.

DISEASE REFERENCE CHART

	What is it?	Cause	Symptoms
Feline Leukaemia Virus (FeLV)	Infectious disease; kills more cats each year than any other feline infectious disease.	A virus spread through saliva, tears, urine and faeces of infected cats; bite wounds.	Early on no symptoms may occur, but eventually infected cats experience signs from depression and weight loss to respiratory distress. FeLV also suppresses immune system, making a cat susceptible to almost any severe chronic illness.
Rabies	Potentially deadly virus that infects warm-blooded mammals.	A bacterium, often carried by rodents, that enters through mucous membranes and spreads quickly throughout the body.	Aggressiveness, a blank or vacant look in the eyes, increased vocalisation and/or weak or wobbly gait.
Feline Infectious Enteritis (FIE) *aka Panleukopenia*	Highly contagious virus, potentially deadly.	Ingestion of the virus, which is usually spread through the faeces of infected cats.	Most common: severe diarrhoea. Also vomiting, fatigue, lack of appetite, severe inflammation of intestines.
Feline Viral Rhinotracheitis (FVR)	Viral disease that affects eyes and upper respiratory tracts.	A virus that can affect any cat, especially those in multiple-cat settings.	Sneezing attacks, coughing, drooling thick saliva, fever, watery eyes, ulcers of mouth, nose and eyes.
Feline Immuno-deficiency Virus (FIV)	Virus that reduces white blood cells.	An infection spread commonly through cat-fight wounds.	Signs may be dormant for years or innocuous, such as diarrhoea or anaemia.
Feline Infectious Peritonitis (FIP)	A fatal viral disease, may be linked to FeLV and FIV.	Bacteria in dirty litter boxes; stress may increase susceptibility in kittens.	Extremely variable; range from abdominal swelling to chest problems, eye ailments and body lesions.
Feline Urological Syndrome (FUS)	A disease that affects the urinary tracts of cats.	Inflammation of bladder and urethra.	Constipation, constant licking of penis or vulva, blood in urine (males), swollen abdomen, crying when lifted.

done by a veterinary surgeon. Both he and you should keep a record of the date of the injection, the identification of the vaccine and the amount given. The first vaccination is normally given when the kitten is about 8–9 weeks old. About 30 days later, a booster is given. Although there are many diseases to which a cat may fall victim, the most dangerous three—FIE, FVR and FeLV—can be safeguarded against with a single (three-in-one) injection. Thereafter, an annual booster is all that is required.

MAJOR DISEASES

There are a number of diseases for which there is either no cure or little chance of recovery. However, some can be prevented by vaccination. All breeders and owners should ensure that kittens are so protected.

FELINE INFECTIOUS ENTERITIS (FIE)
This is also known as feline panleukopenia, feline distemper and feline parvovirus. The virus attacks the intestinal system. It is spread via the faeces and urine. The virus may survive for many years in some environments. The use of household bleach (sodium hypochlorite) for cleaning helps to prevent colonisation. Signs, among others, are diarrhoea, vomiting, depression, anorexia and dehydration. Death may occur within days. A vaccine is available from the vet.

> **A DELICATE HEART**
> A cat's heart is as delicate as a human's heart, but it is much smaller. At full maturity, a queen's heart weighs between 9–12 grammes. The tom's heart is heavier, weighing 11–18 grammes. The blood that circulates through the heart chambers does not supply the heart muscle, thus requiring a separate circulatory system for the heart muscle.

FELINE VIRAL RHINOTRACHEITIS (FVR) & FELINE CALCIVIRUS (FCV)
Also known as cat flu, this is a complex of upper respiratory diseases. Signs are excessively hard sneezing, runny nose and mouth ulcers. Cats vaccinated after having contracted flu may

> **NEUTERING**
> Neutering is a major means of avoiding ill health. It dramatically reduces the risk of males' becoming involved in territorial battles with the dangers of physical injury and disease transference. It makes the male more placid and less likely to scent mark his home. It also reduces the incidence of prostate problems, and there is no risk of testicular cancer. The female avoids potentially lethal illnesses related to her being allowed to remain in an unmated condition, such as breast cancer.
>
> Neutering is usually performed between four and six months of age, but it can be done as early as eight weeks of age. Data available on the age at which a kitten is neutered indicate that early neutering has more advantages than drawbacks. Breeders should have this performed on all cats sold as pets.
>
> Male cats are neutered. The operation removes the testicles and requires that the cat be anaesthetised. Females are spayed. This is major surgery during which the ovaries and uterus are removed. Both males and females should be kept quiet at home for about seven to ten days following the procedure, at which time the vet will remove the sutures.

CARE OF FELINE KIDNEYS

The kidney of the cat is larger than that of the dog, but it has the typical bean shape. It receives 25% of the blood output of the heart! For this reason, it has rather significant veins to accommodate this large supply of blood, and injuries suffered by the kidneys are usually serious and not uncommon.

recover but may suffer from recurrent bouts, especially if they become stressed.

FELINE LEUKAEMIA VIRUS (FeLV)

This is an highly infectious viral disease. It is spread via direct contact—mutual grooming, saliva, feeding bowls, faeces, urine, tears and biting. It can be passed prenatally from a queen to her offspring. It creates tumours, anaemia, immune system depression, pyrexia (high temperatures), lethargy, respiratory disease, intestinal disease and many other potentially fatal problems. It is most prevalent in high-density cat populations. Not all cats will be affected, but they may become carriers.

Kittens less than six months old are especially vulnerable. Infected cats usually die by the time they are three to four years old. Cats can be screened or tested for this disease. Vaccination is not 100% effective but is recommended in kittens being sold into multi-cat environments.

FELINE IMMUNODEFICIENCY VIRUS (FIV)

This causes the white blood cells to be significantly reduced, thus

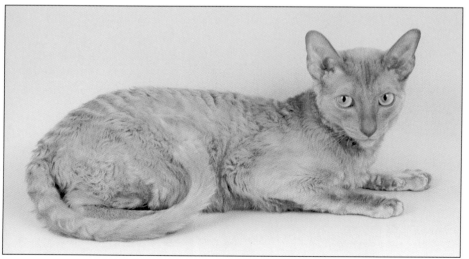

Besides its bond with you, your cat's most important relationship throughout its life will be with the veterinary surgeon.

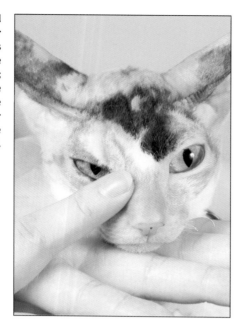

Your vet will check your Cornish Rex's eyes as part of the overall check-up; routine eye checks should be part of your home-care routine as well.

greatly suppressing the efficiency of the immune system. It is not transferable to humans. Infection is normally gained from cat-fight wounds; thus, outdoor males are at the most risk. A cat diagnosed via blood tests as FIV-positive may live a normal life for months or years if retained indoors and given careful attention. Signs may be innocuous in the early stages, such as anaemia or diarrhoea. No vaccine is available.

FELINE INFECTIOUS PERITONITIS (FIP)
This viral disease is invariably fatal once contracted in its more potent forms. However, the virulence of the virus is variable and may by destroyed by the immune system. Stress may increase susceptibility in kittens. It may be linked to FeLV and FIV. Signs are extremely variable and range from abdominal swelling to chest problems, eye ailments to body lesions. There are various tests available but none is as yet 100% conclusive. Strict cleanliness is essential, especially of litter trays. No vaccine is available.

FELINE UROLOGICAL SYNDROME (FUS)
This is a very distressing condition caused by an inflammation of the bladder and urethra. Signs are constipation-like squatting and attempts to urinate, regular licking of the penis or vulva, blood in urine (males), swollen abdomen, crying when lifted and urinating in unusual places (often with only small amounts).

The numerous causes include infection, dirty litter tray of the indoor cat, alkaline urine (in cats it should be acidic), diet too dry, lack of water intake (even though this is available) and being hit by a vehicle (damaged nerves). Veterinary treatment is essential or the condition could be fatal due to the bladder's bursting or the presence of dangerous bacteria.

RABIES
Britain and most European Community countries are free of this terrible disease. The stringent

quarantine laws of Britain are such that vaccination is not necessary. However, the introduction of passports for dogs and cats means that resident British cats must be vaccinated if they are to travel abroad and return to the UK without being placed into quarantine. The vaccination is given when the kitten is three or more months old. The pet passport process takes at least six months to complete, so plan well ahead.

COMMON HEALTH PROBLEMS

Dermatitis (Eczema)

Dry, lifeless coat, loss of coat, tiny scabs over the head and body, loose flakes (dandruff) and excessive scratching are all commonly called eczema. The cause covers a range of possibilities including diet, parasitic mites such as *Cheyletiella spp*, fungus or an allergy to flea or other bites. Sometimes reasons are unknown. Veterinary diagnosis and treatment are required.

Ringworm (Dermatophytosis)

This problem is fungal, not that of a worm. The most common form is *Microsporum canis*, which accounts for over 90% of cases. Cats less than one year of age are at the highest risk, while longhaired breeds are more prone to the problem than shorthaired cats. The fungi feed on the keratin layers of the skin, nails and hair. Direct contact and spores that remain in the environment are the main means of transmission.

Typical signs are circular-type bald areas of skin, which may be flaked and reddish. The coat generally may become dry and lifeless, giving the appearance of numerous other skin and hair

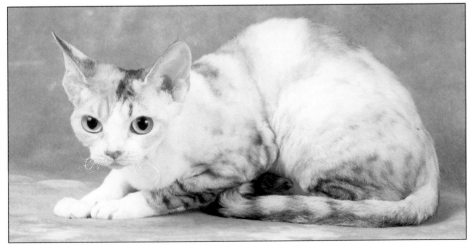

Use grooming time as a time to check your cat's coat and skin for signs of any abnormality, as various types of problems can manifest themselves in these areas.

POSSIBLE SOURCES OF EAR PROBLEMS

- Fight scratches
- Excess secretion of wax
- Swellings and blood blisters (haematoma) resulting from intrusion by foreign bodies (grass, seeds, etc.)
- Sunburn
- Whitish-coloured ear mites (*Otodectes cynotis*)
- Orange-coloured harvest mites (*Trombicula autumnalis*)
- Fleas
- Bacterial infection of either the outer or middle/inner ear

problems. Veterinary diagnosis and treatment, either topical or via drugs, is essential as the condition is zoonotic, meaning that it can be transferred to humans.

EAR PROBLEMS

Most of the common ear problems affect the outer ear. The telltale sign is the cat's constant scratching of the ears and/or its holding the ear to one side. Greasy hairs around the ear, dark brown wax (cerumen) in the ears, scaly flakes in or around the ear and minute white or orange pinhead-like bodies (mites) in the ear are common signs. *Canker* is a term used for ear infections, but it has no specific meaning.

Over-the-counter remedies for ear problems are ineffective unless correct diagnosis has been made. It is therefore better to let the vet diagnose and treat the cat. Some problems may require anaesthesia and minor surgery.

DIARRHOEA

This is a general term used to indicate a semi-liquid to liquid state of faecal matter. Mild to acute cases may be due to a change of environment, dietary change, eating an 'off' item, gorging on a favoured food, stress or a minor chill. These often rectify themselves within days. Chronic and persistent diarrhoea may be the result of specific diseases. Any indication of blood in the faecal matter must be considered dangerous.

In minor cases, withholding food for 12–24 hours, or feeding a simple diet, may arrest the condition. If not, contact your vet. Faecal analysis and blood testing may be required. By answering numerous questions related to the

STRESS TEST
Stress reduces the effectiveness of the immune system. Seemingly innocuous conditions may develop into major problems or leave the cat more open to attack by disease. Stress is difficult to identify specifically, but its major causes are well known. These include incorrect diet, intrusion by another cat in its home or territory, excessive handling and petting, disturbed sleep, uncomfortable home temperatures, bullying by another cat or pet, parasitic infestation, boarding in a cattery, travel, moving, boredom, limited accommodation space and, for some felines, being exhibited.

has damaged the nerves that control bowel movements. As constipation is potentially serious, veterinary advice should be sought. Laxatives and faecal-softener tablets may be given, the faecal matter can be surgically removed or another treatment can be carried out.

CLEANLINESS IS THE KEY
Crucial to the prevention and spread of disease is the need to maintain meticulous cleanliness, especially relating to the litter tray. Many diseases and problems are transferred via faecal matter. Once a problem is suspected, the advice of a vet should be sought. Blood tests, faecal microscopy and other testing methods are now available. They can mean the difference between life and death of a cherished pet.

cat's diet, general health, level of activity, loss of appetite, etc., the vet will determine whether tests are required or if immediate treatment is warranted. Do not give cats human or canine intestinal remedies; these could prove dangerous.

CONSTIPATION
When a cat strains but is unable to pass motions, this is indicative of various causes. It may have hairballs, may have eaten a bird or rodent and has a bone lodged in its intestinal tract, may be suffering from a urological problem rather than constipation, or may have been hit by a car and

EXTERNAL PARASITES

FLEAS

Of all the problems to which cats
are prone, none is more well
known and frustrating than fleas.
Indeed, flea-related problems are
the principal cause for visits to
veterinary surgeons. Flea infestation is relatively simple to cure
but difficult to prevent. Periodic
flea checks for your cat, con-
ducted during annual health
check-ups, are highly recommended. Consistent dosing with
anthelmintic preparations is also
advised. Parasites that are
harboured inside the body are a
bit more difficult to eradicate, but

Flea prevention is
a challenge to cat
owners in most
places. This is an
adult male flea.

they are easier to control.

To control a flea infestation,
you have to understand the flea's
life cycle. Fleas are often thought
of as a summertime problem but
centrally heated homes have
changed the life-cycle patterns,
and fleas can be found at any time
of the year. Fleas thrive in hot and
humid environments; they soon
die if the temperature drops below
2°C (35°F). The most effective
method of flea control is a two-
stage approach: one stage to kill
the adult fleas and the other to
control the development of pre-
adult fleas. Unfortunately, no
single active ingredient is effective
against all stages of the life cycle.

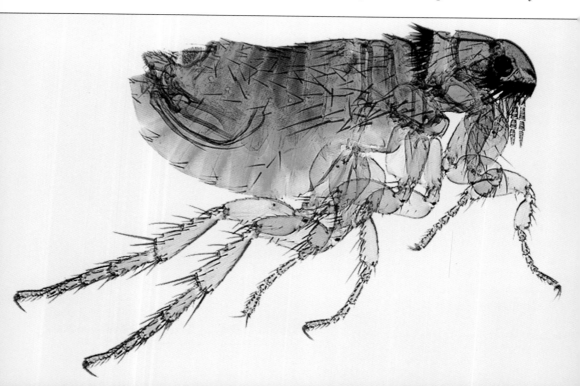

A Look at Fleas

Fleas have been around for millions of years and have adapted to changing host animals. They are able to go through a complete life cycle in less than one month, or they can extend their lives to almost two years by remaining as pupae or cocoons. They must have a blood meal every 10–14 days, and egg production begins within 2 days of their first meal. The female cat flea is very prolific and can lay 2000 eggs in her lifetime!

Fleas have been measured as being able to jump 300,000 times and can jump 150 times their body length in any direction, including straight up. Those are just a few of the reasons why they are so successful in infesting a cat!

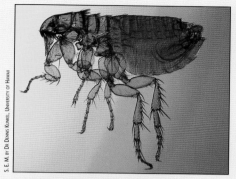

A scanning electron micrograph (S. E. M.) of a flea.

Magnified head of a flea.

LIFE CYCLE STAGES

During its life, a flea will pass through four life stages: egg, larva, pupa and adult. The adult stage is the most visible and irritating stage of the flea life cycle, and this is why the majority of flea-control products concentrate on this stage. The fact is that adult fleas account for only 1% of the total flea population, and the other 99% exist in pre-adult stages, i.e. eggs, larvae and pupae. The pre-adult stages are barely visible to the naked eye.

THE LIFE CYCLE OF THE FLEA

Eggs are laid on the cat, usually in quantities of about 20 or 30, several times a day. The female adult flea must have a blood meal before each egg-laying session. When first laid, the eggs will not cling to the cat's fur, as the eggs are not sticky. They will immediately fall to the floor or ground, especially when the cat moves around or scratches.

Once the eggs fall from the cat onto the carpet or grass, they will hatch into yellow larvae, approximately 2 mms long. This takes from 5 to 11 days. Larvae are not particularly mobile and will usually travel only a few inches from where they hatch. However, they do have a tendency to move away from light and heavy traffic—under furniture, in the carpet and behind doors are common places to find high quantities of flea larvae.

The flea larvae feed on dead organic matter, including adult flea faeces, until they are ready to change into adult fleas. Fleas will usually remain as larvae for around seven days, becoming darker in colour. After this period, the larvae will pupate a protective cocoon. While inside the pupae, the larvae will undergo metamorphosis and change into adult fleas. This can happen within a week, but the adult fleas can remain inside the pupae waiting to hatch for up to six months. The pupae are signalled to hatch by certain stimuli, such as physical pressure—the pupae's being stepped on, heat from an animal's lying on the pupae or increased

Opposite page: A scanning electron micrograph of a flea, magnified more than 100x. This image has been colorized for effect.

> ### FLEA-KILLER CAUTION
> Flea killers are poisonous. You should not spray these toxic chemicals on areas of a cat's body that he licks, on his genitals or on his face. Flea killers taken internally are a better answer, but check with your vet in case internal therapy is not advised for your cat.

carbon dioxide levels and vibrations—indicating that a suitable host is available.

Once hatched, the adult flea must feed within a few days. Once the adult flea finds an host, it will not leave voluntarily. It only becomes dislodged by grooming or the host animal's scratching. The adult flea will remain on the host for the duration of its life unless forcibly removed.

TREATING THE ENVIRONMENT AND THE CAT

Treating fleas should be a two-pronged attack. First, the environment needs to be treated; this includes carpets and furniture, especially the cat's bedding and areas underneath furniture. The environment should be treated with an household spray containing an Insect Growth Regulator (IGR) and an insecticide to kill the adult fleas. There are also liquids, given orally, that contain chitin inhibitors. These

> ### DO NOT MIX
> Never mix flea-control products without first consulting your veterinary surgeon. Some products can become toxic when combined with others and can cause serious or fatal consequences.

A brown tick, *Rhipicephalus sanguineus*, is an uncommon but annoying tick found on cats.

render flea eggs incapable of development. There are also both foam and liquid wipe-on treatments. Additionally, cats can be injected with treatments that can last up to six months. Emulsions that have the same effect can also be added to food. The advanced treatments are only available from veterinary surgeons.

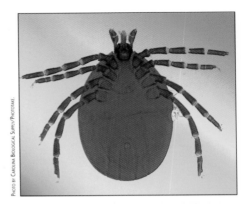

The IGRs actually mimic the fleas' own hormones and stop the eggs and larvae from developing into adult fleas. There are currently no treatments available to attack the pupa stage of the life cycle, so the adult insecticide is used to kill the newly hatched adult fleas before they find an host. Most IGRs are active for many months, while adult insecticides are only active for a few days.

The head of a tick, *Dermacentor variabilis*, enlarged and coloured for effect.

When treating with an household spray, it is a good idea to vacuum before applying the product. This stimulates as many pupae as possible to hatch into adult fleas. The vacuum cleaner should also be treated with a flea

Dwight R Kuhn's magnificent action photo, showing a flea jumping.

treatment to prevent the eggs and larvae that have been hoovered into the vacuum bag from hatching.

The second stage of treatment is to apply an adult insecticide to the cat, usually in the form of a collar or a spray. Alternatively, there are drops that, when placed on the back of the cat's neck, spread throughout the fur and skin to kill adult fleas. A word of warning: Never use products sold for dogs on your cat; the result could be fatal.

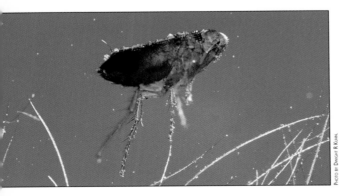

The Life Cycle of the Flea

Eggs

Larvae

Pupa

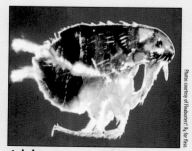

Adult

Flea Control

IGR (INSECT GROWTH REGULATOR)

Two types of products should be used when treating fleas—a product to treat the pet and a product to treat the home. Adult fleas represent 1% of the flea population. The pre-adult fleas (i. e. eggs, larvae and pupae) represent 99% of the flea population and are found in the environment; it is in the case of pre-adult fleas that products containing an Insect Growth Regulator (IGR) should be used in the home.

IGRs are a new class of compounds used to prevent the development of insects. They do not kill the insect outright, but instead use the insect's biology against it to stop it from completing its growth. Products that contain methoprene are the world's first and leading IGRs. Used to control fleas and other insects, this type of IGR will stop flea larvae from developing and protect the house for up to seven months.

EN GARDE:
CATCHING FLEAS OFF GUARD!

Consider the following ways to arm yourself against fleas:

• Add a small amount of pennyroyal or eucalyptus oil to your cat's bath. These natural remedies repel fleas.

• Supplement your cat's food with fresh garlic (minced or grated) and an hearty amount of brewer's yeast, both of which ward off fleas.

• Use a flea comb on your cat daily. Submerge fleas in a cup of bleach to kill them quickly.

• Confine the cat to only a few rooms to limit the spread of fleas in the home.

• Vacuum daily...and get all of the crevices! Dispose of the bag every few days until the problem is under control.

• Wash your cat's bedding daily. Cover cushions where your cat sleeps with towels, and wash the towels often.

Photos courtesy of Fleabusters', Rx for fleas

TICKS AND MITES

Though not as common as fleas, ticks and mites are found all over the tropical and temperate world. They don't bite like fleas; they harpoon. They dig their sharp proboscis (nose) into the cat's skin and drink the blood. Their only food and drink is your cat's blood. Cats can get potentially fatal anaemia, paralysis and many other diseases from ticks and mites. They may live where fleas are found and they like to hide in cracks or seams in walls wherever cats live. They are controlled the same way fleas are controlled.

The tick *Dermacentor variabilis* may well be the most common tick in many geographical areas, especially those areas where the climate is hot and humid. The other common ticks that attack small animals are *Rhipicephalus sanguineus, Ixodes* and some species of *Amblyomma*.

Most ticks have life expectancies of a week to six months, depending upon climatic conditions. They can neither jump nor fly, but they can crawl slowly and can range up to 5 metres (16 feet) to reach a sleeping or unsuspecting animal.

INTERNAL PARASITES

Most animals—fishes, birds and mammals, including cats and humans—have worms and other parasites that live inside their bodies. According to Dr Herbert R Axelrod, the fish pathologist, there are two kinds of parasites: dumb and smart. The smart parasites live in peaceful cooperation with their hosts (symbiosis), while the dumb parasites kill their hosts. Most of the worm infections are relatively

TOXOPLASMOSIS AND PREGNANT WOMEN

Toxoplasmosis is caused by a single parasite, *Toxoplasma gondii*. Cats acquire it by eating infected prey, such as rodents or birds, or raw meat. Obviously, strictly indoor cats are at less risk of infection than cats that are permitted to roam outdoors. Symptoms include diarrhoea, listlessness, pneumonia and inflammation of the eye. Sometimes there are no symptoms. The disease can be treated with antibiotics.

The only way humans can get the disease is through direct contact with the cat's faeces. People usually don't display any symptoms, although they can show mild flu-like symptoms. Once exposed, an antibody is produced and the person builds immunity to the disease.

The real danger to humans is that pregnant women can pass the parasite to the developing foetus. In this case, the chances are good that the baby will be born with a major health problem and/or serious birth defects. In order to eliminate risk, pregnant women should have someone else deal with the litter-box duties or wear gloves while taking care of the litter box and wash hands thoroughly afterwards.

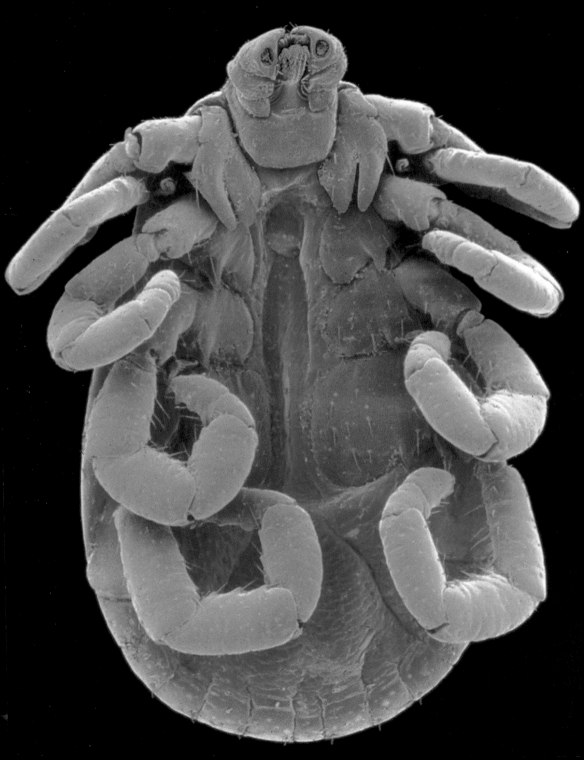

easy to control. If they are not controlled, they weaken the host cat to the point that other medical problems occur, but they are not dumb parasites.

HOOKWORMS

The worm *Ancylostoma tubaeforme* can infect a cat by the larva's penetrating the cat's skin. It attaches itself to the small intestine of the cat, where it sucks blood. This loss of blood could cause iron-deficiency anaemia.

Outdoor cats that spend much of their time in the garden or in contact with soil are commonly infected with hookworm. There is another worm, the *Gordius* or horsehair worm, that, if ingested by a cat, causes vomiting.

TAPEWORMS

There are many species of tapeworms. They are carried by

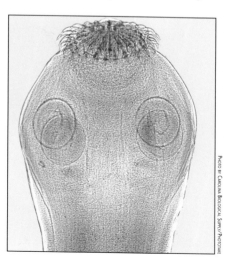

The head and rostellum (the round prominence on the scolex) of a tapeworm, which infects cats and humans.

PHOTO BY CAROLINA BIOLOGICAL SUPPLY/PHOTOTAKE

DEWORMING
Ridding your kitten of worms is VERY IMPORTANT because certain worms that kittens carry, such as tapeworms and roundworms, can infect humans.

Breeders initiate a deworming programme at or about four weeks of age. The routine is repeated every two or three weeks until the kitten is three months old. The breeder from whom you obtained your kitten should provide you with the complete details of the deworming programme.

Your veterinary surgeon can prescribe and monitor the programme of deworming for you. The usual programme is treating the kitten every 15–20 days until the kitten is positively worm-free. It is advised that you only treat your kitten with drugs that are recommended professionally.

fleas! The cat eats the flea and starts the tapeworm cycle. Humans can also be infected with tapeworms, so don't eat fleas! Fleas are so small that your cat could pass them onto your hands, your plate or your food and thus make it possible for you to ingest a flea that is carrying tapeworm eggs.

While tapeworm infection is not life-threatening in cats (smart parasite!), it can be the cause of a

INTERNAL PARASITES OF CATS

NAME	DESCRIPTION	SYMPTOMS	ACQUISITION	TREATMENT
Roundworm (*Toxocara cati* and *Toxascaris leonina*)	Large, white, coil-like worms, 5–10 cms (2–4 inches) long, resembling small springs.	Vomiting, pot belly, respiratory problems, poor growth rate, protruding third eyelids, poor haircoat.	Ingesting infective larvae; ingesting infected mammals, birds or insects; a queen with *Toxocari cati* nursing kittens.	Anthelmintics; scrupulously clean environment (e.g. daily removal of all faeces recommended).
***Physaloptera* species**	2–15 cms (1–6 inches) long, attacks the wall of the stomach.	Vomiting, anorexia, melena.	Eating insects that live in soil (e.g. May beetles).	Diagnosed with a gastroscope; treated with pyrantel pamoate. Prevention of exposure to the intermediate hosts.
***Gordius* or Horsehair worm**	15-cm (6-inch) pale brown worms with stripes.	Vomiting.	May ingest a worm while drinking from or making contact with swimming pools and toilet bowls.	Anthelmintics; avoiding potentially infected environments.
Hookworm (*Ancylostoma tubaeforme*)	The adult worms, ranging from 6 to 15 mms (2.5–6 inches) in length, attach themselves to the small intestines.	Anaemia, melena, weight loss, poor haircoat.	Larva penetrating the cat's skin, usually attacks the small intestine. Found in soil and flower gardens where faecal matter is deposited.	Fortnightly treatment with anthelmintics. Good sanitation (e.g. daily cleanup of litter boxes).
Tapeworm (*Dipylidium caninum* and *Taenia taeniformis*)	Up to 91 cms (3 feet) long. Parts shaped similar to cucumber seeds. The most common intermediate hosts are fleas and biting lice.	No clinical signs—difficult to detect.	Eating infected adult fleas. Uses rodents as hosts.	Praziquantel and epsiprantel. Management of environment to ensure scrupulously clean conditions. Proper flea control.

Magnified heartworm larvae, *Dirofilaria immitis*.

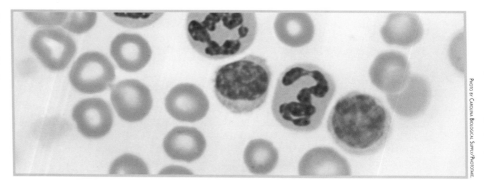

The heartworm, *Dirofilaria immitis*.

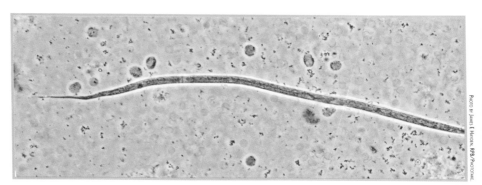

very serious liver disease for humans. About 50% of the humans infected with *Echinococcus multilocularis*, a type of tapeworm that causes alveolar hydatis, perish.

HEARTWORMS

Heartworms are thin, extended worms up to 30 cms (12 ins) long, which are difficult to diagnose in cats as the worms are too few to be identified by the antigen-detection test. Symptoms may be loss of energy, loss of appetite, coughing, the development of a potbelly and anaemia. Heartworm infection in cats should be treated very seriously, as it is often fatal.

Heartworms are transmitted by mosquitoes. The mosquito drinks the blood of an infected cat and takes in larvae with the blood. It takes two to three weeks for the larvae to develop to the infective stage within the body of the mosquito. Cats are less frequently infected with heartworms than dogs are. Also, the parasite is more likely to attack the cat's brain or other organs rather than the heart. Cats should be treated at about six weeks of age and maintained on a prophylactic dose given monthly.

First Aid at a Glance

BURNS/SCALDS
Place the affected area under cool water; use ice if only a small area is burnt. Do not cover the burn or clip hair away. Petroleum jelly can be applied; take cat to vet immediately.

CHEMICAL BURNS
Wash with water only. If you know the chemical is acid, a weak solution of sodium bicarbonate will help, or a vinegar solution will do for alkaline burns.

BEE/INSECT BITES
Apply freshly sliced onion. Apply ice to relieve swelling; antihistamine dosed properly.

ROAD-TRAFFIC ACCIDENT
Move cat from roadway with blanket; seek veterinary aid.

ANIMAL BITES
Clean any bleeding area; apply pressure until bleeding subsides; go to the vet.

SHOCK
Calm the cat, keep him warm and in a horizontal position; seek immediate veterinary aid.

SPIDER BITES
Use cold compress and a pressurised pack to inhibit venom's spreading.

NOSEBLEED
Apply cold compress to the nose; apply pressure to any visible abrasion.

ANTIFREEZE POISONING
Induce vomiting with hydrogen peroxide. Seek *immediate* veterinary help!

BLEEDING
Apply pressure above the area; treat wound by applying a cotton pack.

FISH HOOKS
Removal best handled by vet; hook must be cut in order to remove.

HEAT STROKE
Move animal to cool, shaded area, wet animal with water and place ice packs around head and body; seek immediate veterinary aid.

SNAKE BITES
Pack ice around bite; contact vet quickly; identify snake for proper antivenin.

FROSTBITE/HYPOTHERMIA
Warm the cat with a warm bath, electric blankets or hot water bottles.

ASPHYXIA
Cat must breathe fresh air as soon as possible. Encourage your cat to move around.

ABRASIONS
Clean the wound and wash out thoroughly with fresh water; apply antiseptic.

!! *Remember: an injured cat may attempt to bite an helping hand from fear and confusion. Handle your cat in a calm and gentle manner so as to avoid upsetting the animal further.* !!

THE GERIATRIC CAT

Depending on lifestyle, most cats are considered old at 12 years of age. Some problems that are associated with cats in their veteran years are:

- Decreased energy;
- Intolerance to heat and cold;
- Less meticulous grooming and litter-box habits;
- Decrease in mental alertness;
- Decline of liver and kidney functions;
- Greater susceptibility to diseases, especially dental disease;
- Increased occurrence of cancer.

   As long as owners pay attention and adjust for changing behaviour and diet, and continue regular veterinary care, cats can live well into their teens—some even 20 years and older!

WHAT TO DO WHEN THE TIME COMES

You are never fully prepared to make a rational decision about putting your cat to sleep. It is very obvious that you love your Cornish Rex or you would not be reading this book. Putting a loved cat to sleep is extremely difficult. It is a decision that must be made with your veterinary surgeon. You are usually forced to make the decision when your beloved pet will only suffer more and experience no enjoyment for the balance of its life. Then euthanasia is the right choice.

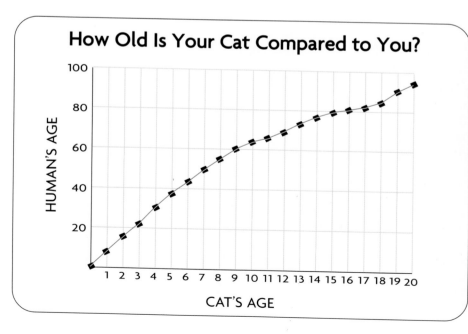

How Old Is Your Cat Compared to You?

WHAT IS EUTHANASIA?

Euthanasia derives from the Greek, meaning *good death*. In other words, it means the planned, painless killing of a cat suffering from a painful, incurable condition, or who is so aged that it cannot walk, see, eat or control its excretory functions.

Euthanasia is usually accomplished by injection with an overdose of an anaesthesia or barbiturate. Aside from the prick of the needle, the experience is usually painless.

MAKING THE DECISION

The decision to euthanise your cat is never easy. The days during which the cat becomes ill and the end occurs can be unusually stressful for you. If this is your first experience with the death of a loved one, you may need the comfort dictated by your religious beliefs. If you are the head of the family and have children, you should have involved them in the decision of putting your Cornish Rex to sleep. Usually your cat can be maintained on drugs for a few days in order to give you ample time to make a decision. During this time, talking with members of your family or even people who have lived through this same experience can ease the burden of your inevitable decision.

THE FINAL RESTING PLACE

Cats can have some of the same privileges as humans. The remains of your beloved cat can be buried in a pet cemetery, which is generally expensive. Alternatively, the cat can be cremated individually and the ashes returned to you. A less expensive option is mass cremation, although, of course, the ashes cannot then be returned. Vets can usually arrange the cremation on your behalf. The cost of these options should always be discussed frankly and openly with your veterinary surgeon. If your cat has died at the veterinary clinic, the vet cannot legally allow you to take the body home, as home garden burials are unlawful.

The remains of your beloved cat can be buried in a pet cemetery.

HOMEOPATHY:
an alternative
to conventional
medicine

'Less is Most'

Using this principle, the strength of an homeopathic remedy is measured by the number of serial dilutions that were undertaken to create it. The greater the number of serial dilutions, the greater the strength of the homeopathic remedy. The potency of a remedy that has been made by making a dilution of 1 part in 100 parts (or 1/100) is 1c or 1cH. If this remedy is subjected to a series of further dilutions, each one being 1/100, a more dilute and stronger remedy is produced. If the remedy is diluted in this way six times, it is called 6c or 6cH. A dilution of 6c is 1 part in 1000,000,000,000. In general, higher potencies in more frequent doses are better for acute symptoms and lower potencies in more infrequent doses are more useful for chronic, long-standing problems.

CURING OUR CATS NATURALLY
Holistic medicine means treating the whole animal as a unique, perfect living being. Generally, holistic treatments do not suppress the symptoms that the body naturally produces, as do most medications prescribed by conventional doctors and vets. Holistic methods seek to cure disease by regaining balance and harmony in the patient's environment. Some of these methods include use of nutritional therapy, herbs, flower essences, aromatherapy, acupuncture, massage, chiropractic, and, of course the most popular holistic approach, homeopathy.

Homeopathy is a theory or system of treating illness with small doses of substances which, if administered in larger quantities, would produce the symptoms that the patient already has. This approach is often described as 'like cures like.' Although modern veterinary medicine is geared toward the 'quick fix,' homeopathy relies on the belief that, given the time, the body is able to heal itself and return to its natural, healthy state.

Choosing a remedy to cure a problem in our cats is the difficult part of homeopathy. Consult your veterinary surgeon for a professional diagnosis of your cat's symptoms. Often these symptoms require immediate conventional care. If your vet is willing and knowledgeable, you may attempt an homeopathic remedy. Be aware that cortisone prevents homeopathic remedies from working. There are hundreds of possibilities and combinations to cure many problems in cats, from basic physical problems such as excessive moulting, hypersensitivity to pain, fleas or other parasites, fever, severe skin problems, upset tummy, obesity, dry, oily or dull coat, diarrhoea, ear problems or eye discharge (including tears and dry or mucousy matter), to behavioural abnormalities such as fear of loud noises, poor appetite, aversion to touch and various phobias. From alumina to zincum metallicum, the remedies span the planet and the imagination…from flowers and weeds to chemicals, insect droppings, table salt and volcanic ash.

Using 'Like to Treat Like'

Unlike conventional medicines that suppress symptoms, homeopathic remedies treat illnesses with small doses of substances that, if administered in larger quantities, would produce the symptoms that the patient already has. While the same homeopathic remedy can be used to treat different symptoms in different cats, here are some interesting remedies and their uses.

Apis Mellifica
(made from honey bee venom) can be used for allergies or to reduce swelling that occurs in acutely infected kidneys.

Calcarea Fluorica
(made from calcium fluoride, which helps harden bone structure) can be useful in treating hard lumps in tissues.

Kali Muriaticum
(made from potassium chloride) can help improve sluggish behaviour.

Natrum Muriaticum
(made from common salt, sodium chloride) is useful in treating thin, thirsty cats.

Nitricum Acidum
(made from nitric acid) is used for symptoms you would expect to see from contact with acids such as lesions, especially where the skin joins the linings of body orifices or openings such as the lips and nostrils.

Symphytum
(made from the herb Knitbone, *Symphytum officianale*) is used to encourage bones to heal.

Urtica Urens
(made from the common stinging nettle) is used in treating painful, irritating rashes.

HOMEOPATHIC REMEDIES FOR YOUR CAT

Symptom/Ailment	Possible Remedy
ABSCESSES	Ferrum Phosphoricum 1.5c, Ledum 1.5c, Echinacea Angustifolia, Silicea 3c
ALLERGIES	Apis Mellifica 30c, Astacus Fluviatilis 6c, Pulsatilla 30c, Urtica Urens 6c
ALOPAECIA	Alumina 30c, Lycopodium 30c, Sepia 30c, Thallium 6c
BLADDER PROBLEMS	Thlaspi Bursa Pastoris, Urtica Urens 3c, Apis Mellifica 1.5c, Rhus Toxicodendron 3c
CONSTIPATION	Alumina 6c, Carbo Vegetabilis 30c, Graphites 6c, Nitricum Acidum 30c, Silicea 6c
COUGHING	Aconitum Napellus 6c, Belladonna 30c, Hyoscyamus Niger 30c, Phosphorus 30c
DIARRHOEA	Arsenicum Album 30c, Aconitum Napellus 6c, Chamomilla 30c, Mercurius Corrosivus 30c
DRY EYE	Zincum Metallicum 30c
EAR MITES	Thyme (Thymus Vulgaris), Rosemary (Rosemarinus Officinalis), Rue (Ruta Gravedens)
EAR PROBLEMS	Aconitum Napellus 30c, Belladonna 30c, Hepar Sulphuris 30c, Tellurium 30c, Psorinum 200c
EYE PROBLEMS	Borax 6c, Aconitum Napellus 30c, Graphites 6c, Staphysagria 6c, Thuja Occidentalis 30c
FVR (Feline Viral Rhinotracheitis)	Ferrum Phosphoricum 3c, Kali Muriaticum 3c, Natrum Muriaticum 3c, Calcarea Phosphorica 3c
GLAUCOMA	Aconitum Napellus 30c, Apis Mellifica 6c, Phosphorus 30c
HEAT STROKE	Belladonna 30c, Gelsemium Sempervirens 30c, Sulphur 30c
HICCOUGHS	Cinchona Deficinalis 6c
INCONTINENCE	Argentum Nitricum 6c, Causticum 30c, Conium Maculatum 30c, Pulsatilla 30c, Sepia 30c
INSECT BITES	Apis Mellifica 30c, Cantharis 30c, Hypericum Perforatum 6c, Urtica Urens 30c
ITCHING	Alumina 30c, Arsenicum Album 30c, Carbo Vegetabilis 30c, Hypericum Perforatum 6c, Mezerium 6c, Sulphur 30c
LIVER PROBLEMS	Natrum Sulphuricum 1.5c, Bryonia 3c
MASTITIS	Apis Mellifica 30c, Belladonna 30c, Urtica Urens 1m
PENIS PROBLEMS	Aconitum Napellus 30c, Hepar Sulphuris Calcareum 30c, Pulsatilla 30c, Thuja Occidentalis 6c
RINGWORM	Plantago Major, Hydrastis Canadensis, Lavendula Vera, Sulphur 3c
UNDERWEIGHT CATS	Medicago Sativa, Calcarea Phosphorica 3c
VOMITING	Ipecac Root 1.5c, Ferrum Phosphoricum 3c

Recognising a Sick Cat

Unlike colicky babies and cranky children, our feline charges cannot tell us when they are feeling ill. Therefore, there are a number of signs that owners can identify to know that their cats are not feeling well.

Take note for physical manifestations such as:

- unusual, bad odour, including bad breath
- excessive moulting
- wax in the ears, chronic ear irritation
- oily, flaky, dull haircoat
- mucous, tearing or similar discharge in the eyes
- fleas or mites
- mucous in stool, diarrhoea
- sensitivity to petting or handling
- licking at paws, scratching face, etc.

Keep an eye out for behavioural changes as well including:

- lethargy, idleness
- lack of patience or general irritability
- lack of appetite, digestive problems
- phobias (fear of people, loud noises, etc.)
- strange behaviour, suspicion, fear
- coprophagia
- whimpering, crying

Get Well Soon

You don't need a DVR or a BVMA to provide good TLC to your sick or recovering cat, but you do need to pay attention to some details that normally wouldn't bother it. The following tips will aid kitty's recovery and get it back on its paws again:

- Keep its space free of irritating smells, like heavy perfumes and air fresheners.
- Rest is the best medicine! Avoid harsh lighting that will prevent your cat from sleeping. Shade it from bright sunlight during the day and dim the lights in the evening.
- Keep the noise level down. Animals are more sensitive to sound when they are sick.

- Be attentive to any necessary temperature adjustments. A cat with a fever needs a cool room and cold liquids. A queen that is birthing or recovering from surgery will be more comfortable in a warm room, consuming warm liquids and food.
- You wouldn't send a sick child back to school early, so don't rush your cat back into a full routine until it seems absolutely ready.

USEFUL ADDRESSES

GREAT BRITAIN
The Governing Council of the Cat Fancy (GCCF)
4-6 Penel Orlieu, Bridgwater, Somerset, TA6 3PG
Email: GCCF_CATS@compuserve.com   Fax: 01278 446627 Tel: 01278 427575

The Cat Association of Britain
Mill House, Letcombe Regis, Oxon OX12 9JD   Tel: 01235 766543

EUROPE
Federation Internationale Feline (FIFe)
Gen. Sec: Ms Penelope Bydlinski
Little Dene, Lenham Heath, Maidstone, Kent ME17 2BS, GB
Email: penbyd@compuserve.com   Fax: 1622 850193 Tel: 1622 850908

World Cat Federation
Hubertsrabe 280, D-45307, Essen, Germany
Email: wcf@nrw-online.de   Fax: 201-552747 Tel: 201-555724

AUSTRALIA
The Australian Cat Federation, Inc.
PO Box 3305, Port Adelaide, SA 5015
Email: acf@catlover.com   Fax: 08 8242 2767 Tel: 08 8449 5880

CANADA
Canadian Cat Association (CCA)
220 Advance Boulevard, Suite 101, Brampton, Ontario L6T 4J5
Email: office@cca-afc.com   Fax: 99050 459-4023 Tel: 99060 459-1481

SOUTH AFRICA
Cat Federation of Southern Africa
PO Box 25, Bromhof 2154, Gauteng Province, Republic of South Africa

USA
American Cat Association (ACA)
8101 Katherine Avenue, Panorama City, CA 91402
Fax: (818) 781-5340 Tel: (818) 781-5656

American Cat Fanciers Association (ACFA)
PO Box 203, Point Lookout, MO 65726
Email: info@acfacat.com   Fax: (417) 334-5540 Tel: (417) 334-5430

Cat Fanciers Association, Inc. (CFA)
PO Box 1005, Manasquan, NJ 08736-0805
Email: cfa@cfainc.org   Fax: (732) 528-7391 Tel: (732) 528-9797

Cat Fanciers Federation (CFF)
PO Box 661, Gratis, OH 45330
Email: Lalbert933@aol.com Fax: (937) 787-4290 Tel: (937) 787-9009

The International Cat Association (TICA)
PO Box 2684, Harlingen, TX 78551
Email: ticaeo@xanadu2.net Tel: (956) 428-8046